Screw

the

Eggshells

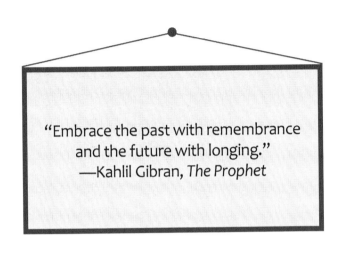

"Embrace the past with remembrance
and the future with longing."
—Kahlil Gibran, *The Prophet*

Finding My *Self* After Verbal and Emotional Abuse

Karen Heckman Stork

Diamond Beach
Press, LLC

Lincoln, Nebraska

SCREW THE EGGSHELLS: FINDING MY *SELF* AFTER VERBAL
AND EMOTIONAL ABUSE

For publishing inquiries, contact:
Diamond Beach Press
c/o Concierge Marketing
4822 South 133rd Street
Omaha, NE 68137
(402) 884-5995

Paperback ISBN: 978-0-9989083-2-8
Mobi ISBN: 978-0-9989083-3-5
EPUB ISBN: 978-0-9989083-4-2
Audio ISBN: 978-0-9989083-5-9

Publishing and production services by Concierge Marketing Inc.
Library of Congress Cataloging Number: 2017940171
Cataloging-in-Publication data on file with the publisher.

Printed in the USA
10 9 8 7 6 5 4 3 2

This book is dedicated to the four most important people in my life: my daughter and best friend whose birth gave my life a purpose; my two grandchildren who have grown up to be caring and productive adults; and, finally, my love who has accompanied me on my journey for the past twenty-five years. I am blessed to have these wonderful people with me on my pilgrimage; they have taught me so much, and through them I have learned so much about myself.

Contents

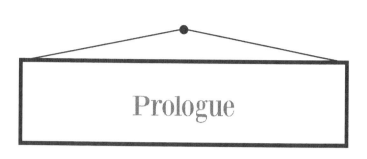

Prologue

HEMINGWAY ONCE SAID ABOUT WRITING, *"All you have to do is write one true sentence. Write the truest sentence that you know."* So that's how I shall begin.

I am seventy-three years old and yet inside I still see myself as a forty-three-year-old woman whose soul longs for the beach.

If you are someone younger than sixty, you're probably thinking "huh?" and "How can she feel that way?" I thought exactly that in the 1990's when my mother, then in her seventies, told me the same thing.

Wanting to spend some "girl time" with her after my father's recent death, I had just taken Mom to a presentation about feminism by Gloria Steinem. I felt my mother needed to reach out and see a different viewpoint on women's lives. (Clearly, I thought I knew more than she did.)

As a social activist, writer, editor and lecturer, Steinem had been an outspoken champion of women's rights since the late 1960's. She was often quoted as saying "a woman needs a man like a fish needs a bicycle," although she says the quote originated with Australian Irina Dunn.

After the presentation, Mom and I sat in the car outside her house discussing some of the "big" questions Ms. Steinem had raised about women's lives. One of Mom's statements flabbergasted me: although she was crippled with arthritis, inside she still felt like a young woman—vibrant, curious, full of energy. Though she couldn't continue to enjoy herself as she had when she was younger, she was not unhappy, but never before had thought about how she felt inside; she'd been too busy being a mother and then taking care of my dad for the last twelve years of his life.

I didn't understand how she could feel so differently on the inside from how she looked on the outside. After all, Mom was old, she had wrinkles and arthritis. How could she still see herself as a young woman who had dreams and plans? I was judgmental then because I hadn't completely learned about life and what it felt like to grow older. Now, after the passage of time and many lessons learned through experience, I know what she meant.

As we talked, out of the blue, my Mom also blurted out, "You know, your Dad never told me that he loved me since we've been married."

I was astounded. How could two people be married for over fifty years without saying those intimate words to each other? But then I thought about my own former marriage, and how those same loving words had been twisted, spoken not to convey feeling, but to control behavior. It was after this discussion with my mother that I began to think about my life of ups and downs, joy and sadness, and where it had led me. And the idea of writing my memoir began as a speck in some nether region of my brain where it marinated and grew and moved until it finally reached the forefront of my mind. Now I am ready to open up my soul, dust off my memories, and talk about my experiences—some trivial, some consequential, and some life-changing. Writing this book has given a voice to my soul.

As we age, our expectations and the things we know "for sure" change because of new insights and life experiences. As a twenty-something-year-old, what I thought was extremely romantic, I later learned at forty was simply a method of control. I experienced controlling behavior as well as verbal and emotional abuse in my marriage. These behaviors increased incrementally over the years until suddenly there was an eruption of anger and emotion. Such episodes eroded my self-confidence and made me doubt my intelligence and question my beliefs.

It took me twenty years to realize how destructive verbal abuse can be. Merriam-Webster defines verbal abuse as "harsh and insulting language directed at a person." I would add the following actions to the definition: insulting remarks, sarcastic jokes and hurtful teasing, and barbed criticisms. Most people dealing with such behavior only smile and laugh along, even though they are the target. Those who have experienced verbal and emotional abuse know that it usually begins slowly with seemingly good-natured joking. However, the person on the receiving end of such "jokes" and insults usually cannot retaliate with words, for fear of escalation of the verbal abuse into physical violence, or because they think they deserve it.

I have two goals in mind for this book. It's more than just relating my life's story. First, I want my story to serve as a cautionary tale. I hope my words and experiences will increase the awareness of other women in similar abusive (though not yet physically abusive) situations and help them find their own way out the other side.

My hope is that young women value their own worth and not give away any of their hopes and dreams to someone who may not truly understand them or deserve their love.

My other goal is for those of us "of a certain age." I want others of the Baby Boomer Generation and older to realize that you are never too old to dream, set goals, or experience new adventures. Have something to look forward to. Continue to work on what you truly love. I believe it's often the "settling for" mentality which leads to stagnation and an early decline.

Before I begin my story, however, I first want to mention why the beach and ocean are so meaningful to me. The beach is my place of sanctuary, a place where I feel most connected to the universe. I discovered my affinity for that particular landscape in the 1990s when, for the first time, I dipped my toes into the great Pacific Ocean. That touch awakened a feeling deep inside me. In that one moment at the ocean's edge, I was inexplicably and forever drawn to the wide and deep watery expanse and the sandy shore.

I've never heard this longing better explained than in a speech by John F. Kennedy given at the dinner for the America's Cup Crews, September 14, 1962: "We all came from the sea. And it is an interesting biological fact that all of us have in our veins the exact same percentage of salt in our blood that exists in the ocean, and, therefore, we have salt in our blood, in our sweat, in our tears. We are tied to the ocean. And when we go back to the sea… we are going back from whence we came."

The never-ending crash of waves on the beach can be so quiet on a calm day or roar like a beast during a storm. Then there is the music of the wind in the trees and of the whistling grass on the dunes.

Another aspect that draws my soul to the intersection of land and sea is the changing light on the ocean. On sunny days, the sun glistens on the sea like diamonds in a mermaid's blue-green hair. On cloudy days, the light is dull and gray, almost misty as with tears.

And finally, there is nothing so awe-inspiring as seeing the sun rise above the ocean, gradually proclaiming the beginning of another day of life on this blue planet. That reverential feeling is only equaled at the end of the day, watching a fiery sunset as the earth's lightbulb slowly sinks behind the horizon, and the earth awaits the moon's nightlight—the darkness signaling a time of rest.

And yet after discovering my psychic connection to the sea, I didn't move to be near the ocean. Because of circumstances which will be explained, I remained land-locked in Nebraska. In my later years, I have tried to visit the ocean as often as possible, but never enough. And when I am gone from this life, I have asked to have a portion of my ashes joined with the deep blue sea, at my sanctuary, my favorite beach, so that my spirit may ever be part of the never-ending cycle of the sea, the moon, and the tides.

Okay, that explains my affinity for the sea, but what does that have to do with my life's story? I really can't answer that question. It just helps explain how I look at life and what's important to me. I am a Pisces, after all, a water sign represented by a fish, the oldest soul in the Zodiac.

In writing this book, I've taken my own advice by continuing to do what I love. Becoming an author has fulfilled one major dream. However, many unanswered questions about my past journey may never be resolved. But that's okay. I no longer believe we can understand everything about our past; we simply must accept that whatever happened got us to where we are now.

And so, let the journey begin.

On the beach in Panama City Beach, Florida, 2016.

Part I

Over Not Easy

"Every decision brings with it some good,
some bad, some lessons, and some luck.
The only thing that's for sure is that indecision
steals many years from many people
who wind up wishing they'd just had
the courage to leap."
—Doe Zantamata

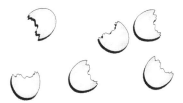

Questions and Doubts

Chapter

1

"A life spent making mistakes is not only more honorable, but more useful than a life spent doing nothing."
—George Bernard Shaw

MY STORY BEGINS AT THE CROSSROADS OF my life—the end of what I was, and the start of a new path. It was a time of learning, understanding, determination and, finally, decision. I shall try, as Hemingway also directed, to "write hard and clear about what hurts."

The year was 1983; I was forty years old and my daughter, Jenny, was twelve. The decade began auspiciously on an exciting and hopeful note. I'd heard about a writing contest sponsored by Young Mothers of Nebraska Association. The subject was, of course, motherhood. I had always felt inside like a writer, but never took the opportunity to pursue my dream. I decided to throw caution to the wind and enter the contest with a story entitled "Loving Her by Letting Go—Learning to Live With a Twelve-Year-Old Daughter."

I needed a reason to return to writing and especially loved telling stories about my daughter, so it didn't take much for me to be convinced to try writing again. I have always liked writing non-fiction stories based on my family background or current situation, though I hadn't had much time to hone my personal writing skills what with raising a daughter and working full-time. Anyway, I decided to give it a try and write about what I knew—what it's like to live with a preteen.

I simply couldn't believe it when a letter arrived telling me that I had actually won the contest and would receive a monetary prize as well as a plaque which would be presented at a recognition dinner for young Nebraska mothers. I was so proud of my accomplishment, and wanted to continue learning more about writing and grammar in hopes of finding a path back to my first love.

Back to College

That contest was the inspiration for me to go back to school and earn my degree in English. I returned to college in 1984. Because I was also working at the University of Nebraska-Lincoln, I could attend up to fifteen hours of classes per year at a cost of only $1 per credit hour. It took me four years to complete the final two years of college.

Those four years back in college were the highlight of my forties. While other areas of my life were imploding and falling apart, my education was a liberating experience. I was apprehensive about being the oldest student in class. *Would other students in class talk to me? Would they know more than I did?* All of my youthful insecurities returned with a vengeance. It had been such a long time since I'd been in a classroom, I wondered how my store of knowledge would match up with kids half my age who were used to the college atmosphere.

I worried for nothing. After much trepidation, I discovered that I loved being in class with students twenty years my junior. I learned a great deal from them, and I like to think that they benefited from interacting with someone of mature years. I always felt accepted and loved learning. I still have many of my school books from those years, and reading is one of my favorite hobbies.

I don't remember my favorite English teacher's name (one of the symptoms of aging), but I do remember some of her axioms for writing. One that still influences the way I write is her rule: "Never start a sentence with 'there is' or 'there are.'" For example, "There is a man watching me from across the street." The better and more active way to draw a picture is to say, "A man is watching me from across the street."

Another rule she taught her students was "show, do not tell" when you are drawing a picture with words. That rule was particularly difficult for me, and virtually every other writer I meet. I always give extra attention to this rule when I'm trying to convey a feeling or situation with words. I was so happy and fulfilled being back in the classroom, learning and writing.

Another of my favorite classes was a comparison of the writings of Hemingway and Fitzgerald, and they remain two of my favorite authors.

This educational interlude was so beneficial for me. I learned much more than just grammar and writing. From

Graduation from the University of Nebraska-Lincoln.

reading and studying various authors and books, I learned about life and its endless possibilities. I firmly believe that my continuing education prepared me for the upcoming hardships that were to follow. At age forty-five, on December 22, 1988, I graduated with a major in English and earned a Bachelor of Arts degree with High Distinction (Magna Cum Laude).

Meanwhile, Back Home

Even as I was enjoying returning to school and getting back to writing at college, my personal life was deteriorating. I had married Ron at age twenty-one when I was naïve and innocent. In that decade of my forties, the decline of our marriage was accelerating, and we grew further apart as I spent more time working. When I was at home, I spent hours studying and writing class papers, as well as spending as much time as I could with my daughter, who was then a teenager.

Ron questioned everything I did and everywhere I went when we weren't together. I felt like an suspect under the glare of that intense light in a police interrogation room. I came to understand that he was probably jealous of what I was accomplishing on my own because he didn't seem happy with his job or the path his life was taking. I tried to encourage him to go back to his art, and see what he could accomplish in that field, but he was not willing to try. He also continued to insist that he "couldn't live without me" and that I wasn't living up to our marriage vows by being gone so much. The constant control, questioning, and distrust were difficult for me to handle. I developed a coping mechanism of walking on eggshells around Ron, doing whatever I had to so as not to upset him. I learned over the years how to tiptoe around his anger instead of actually discussing and confronting our problems.

I began having a separate life from my marriage because I didn't want to destroy my daughter's stability. I was unhappy, but didn't know how to improve our communication or how to solve the problems in our marriage. The more I learned in school and the more I excelled at work, the more my confidence and awareness were growing. I believe my self-image was expanding and changing because my life now included a daughter who looked to me for direction about how a woman interacts in a relationship with another person. I wanted her to see a strong, confident woman who could take care of herself and make her own decisions. However, this new realization didn't lead me to make good decisions at first.

I was not blameless in the divorce that was to follow. I experimented with outside flings during this tumultuous time, but they only provided a temporary respite from the pain. I didn't know if I was running away from something (because Ron could never support my growth or accomplishments) or toward something or someone else to make me feel better.

What made me dare to look elsewhere for love and approval when I was so afraid of Ron's wrath?

After continual verbal abuse and put downs, I didn't feel loved anymore. Every human being wants to be loved; it's a universal urge, a life force.

I was confused and in an emotional fog, not knowing where to turn or how to change the path of my life. However, through reading and meetings of an Al-Anon group, I had finally come to understand that Ron was controlling because he was afraid of losing me. And in a catch-22 situation, he couldn't understand that his controlling behavior only pushed me further away. We were engaged in a tug of war—Ron pulling to exert control over my behavior, and me pushing in the opposite direction. It felt like a battle neither of us could win.

Increasingly, I began to accept the reality that Ron suffered from bouts of depression and that he had been self-medicating with alcohol for a long time. He wouldn't listen when I tried to discuss this problem with him. After a short trial with counseling earlier in our marriage, he wouldn't hear of trying it again. He seemed to think it was all my fault (at least that's what I felt), and if only he could force me to do what he wanted, then everything would be better. Besides continuing to tell me that he couldn't live without me, he told me many times that I was the only person who could help him. Of course, this was just another way of exerting control over me.

One example of my husband's mistrust and jealousy involved a celebration with my UNL coworkers for one of our staff who had just received his green card and was on the path to citizenship. He asked us to go out after work to celebrate with him. I told Ron that I was going out for about an hour or so with coworkers to celebrate our colleague's good news. I might have stayed for an hour and a half, but it wasn't that late. I decided on the way home to pick up dinner to save time. I got spaghetti and meatballs at an Italian restaurant. I knew I would again have to walk on eggshells in order to not upset my husband any more than I already assumed he would be; he would not like it that I had been out socializing with friends.

Arriving home, I said, "I stopped to get dinner because I was sure you and Jenny would be hungry when I got home."

Ron said nothing.

I thought he would appreciate not having to wait to eat. Well, I was certainly wrong about that.

Ron exploded and lost his temper.

He screamed, "I am not going to eat from a plastic container! You should have been home to cook."

He took both plastic containers and threw them against the wall and cupboards of the kitchen. Looking like a murder scene with blood everywhere, the spaghetti and red sauce spilled out over the cupboards, the counter tops and the floor.

"I'm going out to get something decent to eat," he informed me.

Of course, that meant he would come home drunk, and that was always a scary time. Jenny and I cleaned up the kitchen and had sandwiches for dinner, just the two of us. Jenny was also getting used to scenes like this at home, and I always tried to assure her that it wasn't her fault and that things would get better. However, I was finally beginning to understand the adage that "what you allow is what will continue."

The incidents of verbal abuse were indeed increasing. With each incident, with each put down, with each outburst, this ball of words he hurled clung to me like pollen blown on the wind builds up when landing on a compliant flower. This avalanche of abuse was taking over my mind; I didn't know how to get away from it and I was slowly fading and sinking beneath its weight.

The Breaking Point

"What you are is what you
have been, and what you will be
is what you do now."
—Buddha

IN 1987, WHEN SHE WAS SIXTEEN, WE
decided to buy Jenny her first car, even as we continued to
face growing difficulties and upheavals in our marriage.
The car was a 1964 white Plymouth Valiant with no
power steering or power windows, but she was excited
to have gained some independence. We named the car
"Beulah" because it was so old-fashioned. I believe Jenny
felt the car was her
ticket to independence
and a way for her to
escape the fighting and
tension increasingly
prevalent at home.

Jenny's car, "Beulah,"
1964 Plymouth Valiant.

Sweet Sixteen

Today you're "sweet sixteen" and almost grown,
No longer will you be my little girl.
You're searching for the woman you'll become
Who's just about to give her life a whirl.

You've turned into a beauty without braces,
But then I always knew that you would be
Because you are so special and enchanting
And someday soon a boyfriend will agree.

No longer do you need me as a chauffeur,
With "Beulah" you can drive just as you please.
You choose your clothes and put on your own make-up,
No longer do I patch up your scraped knees.

Your eyes are filled with radiant expectation
Awaiting all the joys that life can bring.
You'll soon discover life is an adventure,
Its changing melody is yours to sing.

You're filled with questions I can't always answer,
You'll have to find a path that's right for you.
But just remember that I'll always be here
To lend support in everything you do.

You're growing up so fast and always changing,
From tennis shoes to high heels for the prom.
It's such a joy to have you as a daughter,
You make me very proud to be your Mom.

Jenny's new car was probably the only good thing to come out of that particular year. Ron and I were speaking less and less and avoiding each other more and more. Ron spent many nights out with friends drinking. He followed a particular pattern. If he came home drunk and yelled at me or made a scene, he would always apologize sweetly the next day, often bringing flowers home. He seemed to believe that was all that was necessary for me to forgive his drinking and angry outbursts.

I was nearing the breaking point, and was tired of living two separate lives and not knowing how to fix it. I had always been a meek and accepting person. I never felt I had any options except continuing the marriage. However, in one eventful night, I finally discovered my voice and made myself heard.

I Saw the Light

On a Wednesday night in the fall of 1987, I reached my breaking point—the straw that, as the saying goes, finally broke the camel's back. As usual, Ron was out drinking. Otherwise, the day was a normal day. I had gone to bed at the normal time, around 10:30 p.m. Jenny was sleeping in her room in the lower level of our home.

I was awakened suddenly by a noise and looked at the clock. It was after 2:00 a.m. I trembled, but tried to lay perfectly still in bed, surrounded by my protective eggshells. Ron stumbled awkwardly into the bedroom. I had never been afraid of him before, but for some reason this night I felt paralyzed with fear. My breathing quickened, and my forehead was covered with sweat. I pretended to be asleep.

Suddenly, Ron started bellowing and out of nowhere began calling me every filthy name he could think of.

"Bitch.
Filthy whore.
Sneaky mother f***."**

He said the awful "c word" over and over.

He shouted questions at me:

*"What have you
been doing?"*

*"Where do you really go
when you're not here?"*

"What do you want from me?"

And many more. This name calling and questioning went on and on.

My first reaction was guilt, of course, so I didn't stir; I didn't defend myself.

I didn't say a word. As I lay there, the future unfolded before me—more of the same, more cuts and pinpricks of abuse, never-ending, like the drip, drip, drip of Chinese water torture. Deep inside me, the dam of perseverance and acceptance finally broke.

Screw walking on eggshells! I knew it was over. I could not live like this for one more moment.

Finally, I snapped and jumped out of bed. I believe I surprised him. I was quiet and calm with my anger like a ball of molten lava bubbling up inside my belly.

"No more. You will not call me names any more. I will not be controlled any longer. Get out of this house NOW," I said emphatically.

I was firm and unbending. I don't know where I got the strength or courage to finally stand up for myself. I told Ron to go home to his mother, and he could retrieve his clothes tomorrow.

I don't think Ron knew what had happened. That was so unlike me. He continued to curse as I followed him down the steps and out the front door. I was scared he would attack me, but he didn't touch me. I stood in the open door and watched as his tires screeched and he drove away. My feelings were all over the map. I was sad our family was broken up (and I was sure the marriage was over no matter what Ron said or did), yet elated that I had finally asserted myself. This part of my life was over.

Suddenly, Jenny ran up the stairs. She had heard everything. She had stayed in her room until she knew Ron was gone. She ran into my arms, and we cried together.

"I'm so sorry you had to hear this," I said quietly. "I'm so sorry that your life will now be forever changed."

Jenny didn't utter a word. Her eyes were filled with tears, confusion, and sadness; she clung to me as if I were a life raft in a turbulent sea. In just a few short minutes, the life I had known for twenty-three years was over.

Divorce and Bankruptcy

3

"You have to realize that nothing you have been through was ever wasted. Your past experiences, good and bad, have deposited something on the inside of you. Those challenges sharpened you to help make you who you are today."
—Peter Nielsen

RON DID GO HOME TO LIVE WITH HIS mother. But he continued to return to the house we had shared. He begged for another chance. I said, "No, never again. I want a divorce."

He continued to drink and call almost every day.

A girlfriend of mine came over to help me pack up Ron's possessions and get them out of the house. She was in another room. I didn't hear Ron come in the door, but all of a sudden, my friend was screaming. I ran into the room to see what was happening. Ron was choking her with his hands around her neck. His eyes were glazed over like he didn't even know what he was doing.

"Get out of my house," Ron said to her.

I yelled at him, "Stop or I'll call the police." I dialed 911, and the police were dispatched.

"The police are coming, and you are going to jail," I screamed.

He did let go and stumbled drunkenly out of the house. I couldn't believe this was the same man I had married twenty-three years ago. When the police arrived, I told them what had happened, and where to find Ron. I discovered later that they went over to his mother's house and talked to him. He was not arrested but was told to leave me alone. My entire life was falling apart, but at last I was certain I was doing the right thing.

A few weeks later, things went from bad to really bad. I got a call from Ron's brother. He quietly told me, "Ron took pills and tried to kill himself. He's in the hospital having his stomach pumped."

Ron was unconscious with tubes and IVs attached to every part of his body. His recovery looked bleak. However, after a few days of uncertainty, he did finally wake up and recovered with no lasting effects. He remained in the hospital another couple of days, and his hospital and doctor bills totaled over $35,000 (that was a huge sum in the 1980s). We had no money to pay the bills. We had to declare bankruptcy, and I had to be included because we were still married.

I cannot explain what an awful time this was. My emotions were on a constant roller coaster ride of guilt, anger, sadness and uncertainty. I felt guilty and responsible for Ron's suicide attempt, but I did finally realize that for my own health and the safety of my daughter, I had to get away from this toxic relationship.

Ron returned to his mom's house and went back to work. He seemed to have lost some of his anger, but still couldn't understand why I wouldn't take him back. He kept calling me and asking for another chance. I finally quit answering my telephone. We didn't have caller ID in those days, so I figured if someone wanted to talk to me, they would leave a message.

It was early 1988, and I had hired an attorney to proceed with the divorce. Because of the bankruptcy, we had to sell the house where Jenny had grown up and that I had loved. We were dealing with bankruptcy proceedings, a divorce and selling the house. Triple whammy—1988 was definitely one of the worst years of my life.

Jenny was a junior in high school while all this mayhem was happening around her. I don't know how she survived, but I thank God she had the outlet of music where she could excel, just as I had my outlet of going to school and writing.

I had tried to keep my marriage together for my daughter's sake, but perhaps if I had ended it sooner, this period wouldn't have been so dramatic and unsettling for all of us. It's difficult to know what's best when you're going through the chaotic and messy breakup of a marriage.

The medical bankruptcy went to court first and was settled fairly quickly. Jenny and I were preparing the house for sale, and I was proceeding with the divorce. I don't know which came first—the divorce or the sale of the house. I do remember going to court for the divorce. Ron wasn't required to be there and he wasn't. The final divorce decree was granted on October 14, 1988. Our house lingered on the market for some time, but it was finally sold. Thus, ended the most heart-wrenching few years of my life. I had suffered and I had learned.

I had let Ron take over most of my life and my decisions. I didn't always listen to him, but I was afraid to speak my own mind and follow my own life path. I learned that one person was not responsible for another's happiness; we had to each find our own happiness. I finally realized that I had been an accomplice in the demise of our marriage because I had not insisted on my needs and wishes, and I had looked elsewhere for happiness and satisfaction. I had not acted as the captain of my own life's journey. But from that point forward, my future depended solely on me.

Part II

What Came First?

"God gave us our memories so that
we might have roses in December."
—J. M. Barrie

My Childhood and School Years— Growing Up on Washington Street

Chapter

4

"My curfew was lightning bugs. My parents didn't call my cell, they yelled my name. I played outside, not on-line. If I didn't eat what Mom cooked, I didn't eat."
—Unknown

I TRULY BELIEVE that those of my generation, i.e., born in the 1940s and early '50s, were lucky because we were perhaps the last generation to have enjoyed a carefree, innocent childhood during the family-centered era of the 1950s. It seems that everything changed during the 1960s, a decade that brought great upheaval to life in the United States, including good changes like the civil rights movement, but also some negative changes, such as Vietnam, three high-profile assassinations (including President John F. Kennedy), political riots and a loss of childhood innocence.

Cost of Living in 1953

Gallon of Milk: $.94

Loaf of Bread: $.16

Dozen Eggs: $.72

Postage Stamp: $.03

Minimum Wage (hour): $.75

Gallon of Gas: $.22

The average annual income was around $4,000, with a new auto costing $1,850 and a new home costing $17,400.

That's me at one year old.

*My parents married
in September 1941.*

During the 1950s mothers typically stayed home and fathers went to work. Children were not constantly watched, and therefore we learned to solve our own problems and differences. We played games in the street like kick the can, stick ball, hop scotch and hide-and-seek. On Halloween, we went trick or treating in one big group by ourselves— no parents in sight. We didn't have seat belts, cell phones, microwaves, and TVs didn't come to our neighborhood until I was in junior high school.

My story began simply enough in 1943 in a little two-room house behind my maternal grandparents' home that was called "The Little House" (and this was long before *Little House on the Prairie* was on TV). All of my mom's brothers and sisters began their married lives in that little house. My heritage is German from Russia on both sides of my family. My mom grew up in a neighborhood of Germans from Russia called the North Bottoms, and my father grew up in a similar ethnic neighborhood called the

South Bottoms. I was told that my parents' romance was similar to the story of *Romeo and Juliet*—no one who grew up in the North Bottoms would ever fall in love with and marry someone from the South Bottoms. But they did, and that marriage produced me and my younger brother, Tom.

When I was two years old, our family moved into the home where I lived until I got married, in a block-long series of homes with families like ours. I called them FINKS (Families with One Income and Kids). I grew up with at least twelve other children from six families. The Washington Street gang included Tom and me, Tammy and Vicki, Mike and Scott, Judy and Mike, Don and Susie, and John and Billy.

I grew up on a street called Washington in a town called Lincoln.

In other words, this neighborhood was the all-American typical block of the era. The families on our block were just like *The Adventures of Ozzie and Harriet* and *Father Knows Best* (for those of you who remember the early TV situation comedies), and this scenario was repeated in towns all over the country in post-war America.

The Washington Street gang.

My dad in front of the house where I grew up on Washington Street, circa 1950.

The feeling on Washington Street was one of being part of a small community or a large family with six fathers and six mothers. All kids were welcome in any of the neighbors' houses and were disciplined in the same manner as the kids who lived in that particular home. No permission was needed from other parents; all children were treated the same, as part of each of the six families. And no matter at which house we were playing, if lunchtime came, we were all served lunch together.

I have so many happy memories of my childhood in this idyllic neighborhood. As a typical gang of kids, we ate green apples from an orchard in an empty lot at the end of our street. Railroad tracks ran north and south on the other side of that empty lot. You could set your watch by the trains that rumbled through our neighborhood, and no, we didn't live "on the other side of the tracks." In those days, tracks transversed our city in many different places. In the summer or after school, if we heard the train coming, we'd all run down near the tracks to wave hello to the engineers.

I can still see that empty lot today, filled with volunteer trees and waist-high weeds in the summer. That lot was the Wild West where we played cowboys and Indians; it was a jungle with hidden dangers that we ran from and climbed trees to escape; it was our own personal Disneyland where our imaginations lifted us out of our small world into exotic locales we could never imagine going. In another empty lot across the street, we played baseball all summer long. And in the summer, we only headed home when the sun set, and it was too dark to continue our adventures.

We were also a theatrical group of kids. Each summer in our garage, against the backdrop of a pink chenille bedspread, we staged musical extravaganzas. We set up lawn chairs in our driveway, charged admission and sold lemonade. I can still see clearly in my mind's eye the picture of Jimmy (the only kid older than me in the group) and me singing "How Much is that Doggie in the Window." No, we didn't need TV, cell phones or iPads to put on a production or entertain ourselves. That was the magic of growing up in the fifties.

One summer, our curiosity got us kids into a whole peck of trouble. It was Independence Day, and I was perhaps ten years old, and my brother was eight. Our parents were having a party in the backyard; all the grown-ups were in their bathing suits and drinking beer. My cousins and some of the neighborhood kids were upstairs in my bedroom.

I had many dance recital costumes hanging in my closet (I began taking dance lessons from Donna McCandless when I was five and continued through high school). The question arose about whether or not the costumes were

The Washington Street Parents, circa 1960s. Mom and Dad are front row, second from the left.

flammable. And, of course, my brother and I then had to investigate. We lit a match and held it against one of the costumes in my closet. Of course, it burst into flames.

My brother ran downstairs to tell our folks. They thought he was saying, "There's a big bug upstairs!" It took them a little while to figure out what was happening. In the meantime, I had filled up a bucket in the bathroom and tried to douse the flames. Thank goodness, the fire department arrived, and the incident ended without injury and only minimal damage to my bedroom. Needless to say, we were reprimanded and punished by not being able to leave the house or play with our friends for probably the rest of the summer.

The neighborhood "gang" also stayed in close touch during the school year as well. We all walked to school together—about one-and-a-half miles to and from school, both elementary and junior high (there was no middle school in those days). Because most families had only one car, our moms couldn't chauffeur us to school because dad had to drive the "family" car to work. Yes, we walked in all kinds of weather, including snow and rain. It always took us longer to walk to and from school during inclement weather because we liked to jump in puddles if it was raining and throw snowballs or lay down and make snow angels when it snowed.

A middle point in this trek was a small neighborhood shopping area on Sumner Street with a drugstore, a barber shop, and a few small businesses. We'd stop there on the way home from school to meet up with other neighborhood friends for a chocolate shake from the fountain or to buy candy or magazines. When Tom was in fifth grade, he stole cigarettes from the drugstore for himself and his friend Paul. Nobody ever knew, or so he told me.

I had my first kiss in the sixth grade (which was still in elementary school in the 1950s) on the playground after school. However, I'm not sure which of two boys (Dan or Doug) gave me my first kiss! My first boy-girl party was also in sixth grade, a roller-skating party. The local roller-skating rink was popular in the 1950s, and we went there a lot. I can still clearly hear the organ music and see my younger self rolling effortlessly around the rink in my rented skates. I recently read that Lincoln's family-owned roller skating arena, Skate Zone, which has operated in the same location on 48th Street for over sixty-two years, closed its doors in 2017. So sad to see so many of my childhood memories gone.

Some Family Memories

I have many fond memories of family togetherness during my childhood. I know it must sound like I'm from another planet, but as a kid I looked forward to Sundays with the family.

In the 1950s, we had many family traditions as well as chores and duties. For example, my brother and I were expected to make our beds each morning and do our homework by ourselves each evening before bed. And we didn't have calculators to help with our math homework. We also, of course, didn't have a dishwasher, so we had to take turns clearing the table after dinner and drying the dishes with our mom or dad (they also took turns).

After dinner and after our homework was done, we looked forward to at least one hour of family television time. I was in junior high school when we got our first black and white TV housed in a big blond cabinet—with no remote control either. Some of my favorite shows included

Gunsmoke, I Love Lucy, Father Knows Best, The Adventures of Ozzie and Harriet, and especially on Sunday nights, *The Ed Sullivan Show.*

Another reason that I loved Sunday as a kid was my favorite family summer tradition. We didn't go on many family vacations in the summer; instead our summer Sundays were spent taking mini-vacations in town almost every weekend.

Of course, we continued to go to church and Sunday school in the morning. But immediately after church, we'd race home, shed our Sunday best and slip into our swimsuits. Mom would prepare a picnic lunch to take with us, and dad, mom, Tom and I would head to Capitol Beach amusement park and swimming pool, which was located a few miles west of town, a location that is now covered by Capitol Beach Lake.

Capitol Beach was in operation from 1917 to 1961. By the time we enjoyed the swimming pool in the 1950s, the huge Jack Rabbit roller coaster was no longer in service. However, according to Lincoln historian Jim McKee, at least in the early part of the decade, many other features

Mom, Dad, Tom, and I ready to go to Capitol Beach, circa 1950.

were still up and running. Some of these attractions included the Ferris wheel, merry-go-round, dodge 'em cars and kids' boat ride. My younger brother enjoyed going to the roller skating rink (which was in the same building as the dodge 'em cars).

But our family summer Sundays were spent in the large saltwater swimming pool; it was just like what I expected the ocean to smell, taste and feel like. A sand beach even surrounded the cement pool that made it feel more like a sea shore environment. (Maybe that's when I first developed my affinity for the beach and the sea?)

We had a great time swimming and playing for hours (if my brother and I didn't try to drown each other, that is). Dad would carry us around on his shoulders and then dunk us in the water. Tom and I would race each other across the pool. This could be difficult because the pool was always crowded. Dad loved to show off by doing a fancy dive off the highest diving board, and continue to swim underwater all the way to the other side of the pool.

At the end of the afternoon, before exhaustion took over, the family would head home for a quick dinner. I don't remember the whole family ever eating at a restaurant before our teen years. There were no McDonald's in Lincoln in the 1950s. The first McDonald's opened in Lincoln at 5305 O Street around 1960.

We always ended our idyllic family summer Sunday outings at the Starview Outdoor Theater near 48th and Vine Street. The first drive-in theater in Lincoln, the Starview opened in May 1948 and remained open for almost forty years. In the 1950s, the cost for adults was sixty cents and kids under twelve were free. Before the show, Tom and I would go down to the playground in front of the giant

My brother, Tom, and me at two and four years old.

screen and swing, play on the slides, and run around with other kids. When the sun began to set, we would race back to the car for some homemade snacks including cookies and popcorn. Dad would pick up the huge speaker from its stand next to the driver's window and place it on the open window. The sound reverberated with feedback from the same speaker on every other car's open window throughout the theater. Sometimes we would sit on the back fender of the car and watch the moon and the stars come out. Once it got dark and the film began, Tom and I usually fell asleep in the back seat; we always came prepared for this eventuality with blankets and pillows.

These predictable family Sunday outings are special memories for me today. The memories grow more vivid as time advances, even as many other parts of my past continue fade away into the mist.

Christmas Eve

A most memorable Heckman family tradition was our Christmas Eve celebration. Both sides of my maternal (Kolb) and paternal grandparents were Germans from Russia. All had immigrated to the United States in the early 1900s. The Kolb family came from Laub, Russia, in 1907. They brought all their old-world Christmas traditions with them to their new home in America.

My mom (middle front) with her brothers and sisters and their mom, circa 1970s.

While I was growing up during the 1940s and 1950s, my grandparents retained their German heritage, including food and language. They spoke English, but preferred to speak German at home. My mom and her seven brothers and sisters, however, spoke mainly English and had fully assimilated into the American way of life.

We always spent the night before Christmas at my maternal grandparents' home in the North Bottoms neighborhood of Lincoln with all of Mom's brothers and sisters and their families. It was quite a crowd, even though everyone usually wasn't there at the same time. The North Bottoms was a neighborhood just north of the university's city campus

Wedding of my maternal grandparents, Caroline Johns and Peter Kolb, Jr. on December 12, 1919.

bounded approximately by 6th and 14th Streets. Most Germans from Russia lived in this neighborhood or the South Bottoms which was south of O Street, again bounded approximately by 6th and 14th Streets.

The Kolbs lived as farmers in a city neighborhood. Grandpa raised chickens in an enclosed chicken yard which had brick paths and chicken coops inside a high fence, totally unseen. He raised baby chicks in a heated hatchery, and there were always eggs for breakfast and eventually chickens for dinner. His chicken yard was spotless as he would sweep it every day. It was as clean as the inside of most people's homes. Their yard was full of fruit trees (apples, plums and cherries) which we picked every summer to make pies. Grandma had a large garden in the yard right beside the house and grew most of their vegetables. She made pickles and canned fruit and vegetables for the winter. Their neighbors in the North Bottoms also benefitted from this inner city "farm," and they helped each other through the years of the Great Depression by bartering for goods and services.

For our Christmas celebration, Grandpa always made homemade wine from plums as well as homemade sausage, which was made mostly with pork and included no additives at all. The sleeves of sausage hung from the rafters curing in his attic. My favorite was liver sausage, but Grandpa's homemade variety was the only kind I would eat. I've never eaten liver sausage since Grandpa quit making it. Grandma was also a wonderful cook, and I especially remember her runzas (before they became so well-known), kuga (a kind of crumbly coffee cake) and chicken noodle soup, which always included what we called "butter balls."

On Christmas Eve, most of the family attended church services at the church on 8th and Charleston, only three blocks from our grandparents' home. The children usually stayed home with one or two of mom's younger brothers or sisters to watch us. Since I was the oldest cousin, when I was old enough, I had to watch over the younger cousins while the others were in church.

My grandparents never had a full-size Christmas tree. Their tree was always small and sat on a living room table. After living through the Depression, they retained their frugal ways. When the cousins opened Christmas presents, we discovered such useful gifts as handkerchiefs, socks, or school supplies.

After dinner and presents, my grandparents and some of their children sang Christmas carols from a German carol book. The words were all German, and the singing was a cappella. I can still sing some of the German words to "Silent Night"—"stille nacht, heilige nacht" ("silent night, holy night"). Such a beautiful sound it was. My grandma, my mom, my daughter, and I all inherited good singing voices and we participated in school and church choirs.

Later, some of the brothers and sisters and families would gather at our house on Washington Street. Of course, my brother and I had to go to bed to await the arrival of Santa Claus. The cousins were put to bed in our parents' room. Sometimes when I couldn't sleep, Tom and I would creep down the stairs and look through the spindles to watch all the grown-ups drinking beer and playing cards. But we would soon tire and find our way back to bed and fall asleep while "visions of sugar plums danced in our heads."

Junior High

In 1955, I began attending Irving Junior High School. Many "firsts" happened for me in junior high—first musical performance, first boyfriend, first encounter with a killer in my hometown.

I was a little Munchkin kid in *The Wizard of Oz*. With two or three others, I sang this song to Dorothy just after she landed in the land of Oz:

"We represent the lullaby league, the lullaby league, the lullaby league,
And in the name of the lullaby league,
We wish to welcome you to Munchkin land."

I wanted to play Dorothy, of course, but was happy to be a Munchkin. I still recall all the words and how we looked. This experience was one of my favorite junior high school memories, and it led me into drama and singing in high school. To this day, I still enjoy singing in the church choir or harmonizing along with Willie Nelson on the radio.

Another fond musical moment from junior high that lingers in my memory are bands playing and students dancing in the cafeteria during lunch. We had such carefree fun during those lunchtimes, pre-pubescent tweens and teens. I can still see us all dancing in my mind's eye whenever I hear the song "Peggy Sue." Rock and roll was just beginning, and so many of the songs from the fifties and sixties are evocative of those turbulent, changing times in our lives.

I attended my first musical concert on May 19, 1956, at the end of seventh grade, my first year in junior high. I had just turned thirteen in March. My idol, Elvis Presley, performed in Lincoln, Nebraska, in the University Coliseum, and I was there!

I have no memory of how I managed to go to that concert, but I'm sure some grown-up must have taken me and some of my friends. I can still feel the excitement, hysteria almost, of all the girls in poodle skirts and saddle shoes, screaming as loud as they could. Sometimes it was so loud we couldn't even hear Elvis. I was close to the stage because the concert was general admission with no seats. I still can't believe I was lucky enough to have been there at that momentous musical performance, at the dawn of the rock and roll era. Elvis has always been one of my favorite singers, and his music still makes me nostalgic for a simpler time.

I had my first serious boyfriend in ninth grade. I walked to his home after school, and his mother would then drive me home. These were innocent times, but I'll never forget my first intimate incident with a boy touching my breasts.

We were in my living room alone. He put his arm over my shoulder, and ever so slowly his hand reached further and further down until it was rubbing my breast. Nothing was said, and I didn't know what to do. I was a good girl. I didn't know whether to be horrified, embarrassed, or excited at this "grown-up" move. Before I could decide how to react or before he could remove his hand, my mother entered the room, and the hand was quickly raised to my shoulder. Later my mom and dad sat me down and explained why I should not let a boy touch me in certain places.

Murder in the School Neighborhood

One of my most vivid memories of junior high in the 1950s was a horrific incident which received national news coverage and was immortalized in music, books and film. The year was early 1958 and I was in ninth grade. The characters in this gruesome tale were Charlie Starkweather and Caril Ann Fugate. They were engaged in a deadly murder spree in Nebraska, and one of the couples they shot was Clara and C. Lauer Ward, along with their maid Lillian Fencl. These murders occurred only a few blocks from our junior high school. The Ward's son, who was my age, was away at boarding school and escaped the murderous rampage. The facts of this murder became public on a cold and blustery January school day, and children were not allowed to leave school without a parent. I will never forget the scene of parents arriving at the school armed with shotguns and other weapons.

During the entire ordeal, we were glued to our TVs and radios to find out the latest news. That was the first time I can remember not feeling safe in my hometown and inside my own home. Our entire routine was turned upside down and sideways. Parents began walking their children to and from school. We didn't play outside with other neighborhood kids for many, many weeks. Families spent much more time inside watching television and listening to the radio.

Starkweather and his girlfriend were finally captured in Wyoming after murdering a state trooper there. That would bring the total number of people he had murdered in just two months to eleven. This grisly tale ended only eighteen months later when Starkweather was executed in June of 1959. That's a totally different situation than today when convicted murderers can sit on death row for twenty years or more. The whole town of Lincoln felt safe again as a new decade was just around the corner.

High School High Jinks

Just six months after the Starkweather murder rampage in 1958, I began high school at Lincoln High. This transition can be difficult and unnerving—going from the top of the ladder back down to the bottom rung. LHS was a large school with people of all sizes, shapes, nationalities and colors from so many junior high schools in the city. I was afraid of getting lost, being late to class, not having any friends and not being "cool." It is a universal axiom to want to fit in, especially for teenagers. In recent years, we have seen the awful consequences from some students who felt they didn't "belong." The times were more innocent in the late fifties, but the feelings haven't changed.

My dad had traded his first car, a long black Chevrolet four-door sedan, for a 1954 green and white Chevy in which I learned to drive. I loved that car, and it holds many fond and not-so-fond memories of my teenage years. One unfortunate incident involved one of my girlfriends smoking in the back seat and throwing the stub out the window. Unfortunately, some of the ashes flew back in, nestled in the back seat, and later that evening, while the car was parked in our driveway, a fire broke out. It wasn't a big fire, but it led to a lecture on the evils of smoking and that no one should ever smoke in my car again, or my driving privileges would be rescinded.

I had a wide group of friends, most of whom were considered to be the "in group." High school had many cliques back in the fifties and sixties. However, I had always felt like somewhat of an outsider because my family wasn't rich or connected to the upper echelon in Lincoln, and I was a learning and book nerd. The "in group" was big enough, however, that many different kinds of girls were part of the group, and within the large group were many smaller circles of close friends.

One of the rites of passage for teenage high school girls (though I can't for the life of me understand why) was the obligatory slumber party. However, in high school I certainly went along with the group in this regard. The entire group was never invited to all slumber parties. Depending on who was having a slumber party, the hostess would typically invite from six to ten of her friends to join her.

We did the things girls usually have done at slumber parties for many years; we had lots of food, played games, maybe fixed each other's hair, and especially talked about boys—who was dating whom, what outrageous thing someone had done recently, who had recently broken up, etc. Actually, boys quite regularly would show up at a slumber party. They would sit outside and talk to us, but as far as I can remember (and that isn't very far, as my friends will tell you), boys never came into the house during a slumber party.

One of my most enduring memories of high school slumber parties was at Dixie's house. She described what for her was "one of the greatest feelings in the world," and it involved four things: (1) having just taken a bath/shower and therefore having a clean body, (2) having also washed your hair, (3) putting on a clean nightgown or PJs and (4) getting into a bed with newly washed sheets. Isn't it odd that over fifty years later, I think of Dixie's insight every time those four activities happen to occur on the same night. It's funny what sticks with you and what you forget about the past.

I remember another slumber party that I had at my house. At this particular slumber party, there weren't enough places for everyone to sleep. My bedroom was upstairs, but because there were so many of us, most of the girls chose to sleep in sleeping bags in the living room. Susan, however, woke up sometime during the night and decided to take her pillow and blanket and try to get some sleep in the bathtub. Well, my folks were both home that evening, and when they went to bed, all the girls were in the living room. During the early morning hours, my dad got up and went upstairs to use the bathroom—never realizing that someone was sleeping in the bathtub. It must have awakened Susan because she told the story. The important detail I can't quite recall is if she kept quiet while my dad was in the bathroom or made some noise that alerted him to her presence.

One of our favorite slumber party activities was "TPing" someone's house (covering someone's house and lawn with toilet paper, that is). One of the rules of high school culture was that if your house was never "TPed" by a group of your "friends," then you really weren't popular.

Another fun activity (one usually involving boys also) was "painting the bridge." A particular railroad bridge on 29th and Sumner Street next to Antelope Park was used for this purpose. No one knows how or when the tradition began. In the early 1960s we only had three high schools— Lincoln High, Southeast and Northeast. One of the rituals for seniors was to paint their year of graduation on the bridge in their school colors. Then another group of seniors from rival schools would try to cover up the other school's colors. That bridge painting tradition continued on our twentieth LHS class of 1961 reunion when we, for the last time, painted "the bridge."

One of the most daring things I did in high school (and I certainly was not a person to disobey the rules or norms) was to date a younger guy. In the summer between my junior and senior year, a friend of mine and I dated two boys who were juniors. We all had names for each other. We were known as "The Big Four." I was Hilda Homemaker, my friend was Gertie Gardner, and the boys were Joe Guy and Stu Stud. We drove around in "Stu's" old green coupe which he called The Green Hornet. We went swimming at Fremont lakes, double dated to movies, talked sometimes all night, swam at Muny (Municipal) Pool, and just hung out. We were the scandal de jour for many weeks when school started again. We had broken an unwritten taboo. However, the talk finally subsided and normalcy was restored.

Sometime in my senior year, I dated another junior boy named Phil, and we had a wacky adventure on the night we went to see the new Alfred Hitchcock movie, *Psycho*. Phil's mother worked in the downtown library, so we were able to park his car in the alley next to the library. Those of you who are familiar with that famous movie probably remember the unforgettable shower murder scene. Well, after the movie I was still a little scared walking down the alley to Phil's car. As we neared the car, we noticed two legs hanging out of the front passenger's window. (In those days, you didn't need to roll up the windows or lock your car.) I squeaked out a garbled scream, and Phil pushed me behind him as he went to open the car door. It was just a hobo (as we called transients in those days) who was sleeping. Phil pulled him out of the car, and we got in and went home.

"The Betty"

In my senior year at Lincoln High School, I was lucky enough to be the recipient of a $1,500 college scholarship as the Nebraska statewide winner of the Betty Crocker

Homemaker of Tomorrow contest. This scholarship program ran from 1955 through 1977, and the founders noted that the purpose of the contest was to focus attention on the "forgotten career" of homemaking.

A teacher at Lincoln High School suggested that I sign up for the contest, even though I was not in the high school "homemaking track." I was planning to go to college. The statewide winner's prize was a $1,500 college scholarship, so I was excited to try. The test consisted of a set of 150 multiple choice questions in a number of high school subjects like science, homemaking skills, child care and citizenship. The test also included a required essay question. The topic for the essay was something along the lines of the importance of marriage and family in today's world.

One day a couple of months after taking the test, I received a note summoning me to the office of the Assistant Principal and Dean of Girls, Dorcas Weatherby. That was not a good sign, usually. After arriving in her office, I received the good news that not only had I received the highest score on the test in the city of Lincoln, but I had also won the title of Statewide Winner of the Betty Crocker Homemaker of Tomorrow contest.

As the statewide winner from Nebraska, in addition to the $1,500 scholarship, I would receive an all-expenses-paid trip to Washington, D.C., New York City, and Williamsburg, Virginia. All the statewide winners would continue the competition at a national level for more scholarships. I was lucky enough to have my mother accompany me on this journey since there were no school chaperones who could attend. It was my first airplane ride on a small two-engine jet, and my mother and I were all dressed up with hats and gloves for the trip.

Mom and me, all dressed up for our first airplane ride.

The first stop was New York City, where we stayed in the Hotel Waldorf Astoria. Our first activity as a group of state winners was a bus tour across the city including the United Nations Headquarters, the Empire State Building, and other famous landmarks. In the evening, we got to see the Broadway musical *The Sound of Music* with Mary Martin in the starring role. I still have an autographed program from that show. I made some good friends on the trip, especially with the winners from Montana and Nevada, because when we traveled as a group, we always lined up in state alphabetical order, and those girls were in front of and behind me.

Our next stop was Williamsburg, Virginia, where we toured the historical homes and exhibits and stayed for one night at the historical Williamsburg Inn. We took a carriage

Betty Crocker Homemaker of Tomorrow state winners.
I am in the second row, second from the left.

ride, bought souvenirs, and had a wonderful time.

The final stop and highlight of the trip was a visit to Washington, D.C. where we toured the Capitol Building, the White House, and other historical monuments. Our last event was a formal dinner with the senators from our states. The Nebraska senators at that

I'm all dressed up for formal dinner with Senator Carl Curtis (R-NE) in 1961.

time were Roman Hruska and Carl Curtis. I had my picture taken with Senator Curtis in my strapless yellow formal and wrist corsage.

Although I didn't win any additional scholarships, the trip was and still is one of the highlights of my life. I was especially pleased that my mother got to accompany me and share in my first "adult" adventure.

My Future Beckons

In the latter part of my senior year, I met my future husband, Ron, and my whole life changed. At that time, Ron was dating a cheerleader who was one of my friends, and I was dating another guy in the "group." One particular Saturday, there was an out-of-town football game, and the cheerleaders were in attendance. The details have faded from memory, but some of us who didn't go to the game ended up with the group of about six guys who always hung out together. I knew that most of the guys in this "group" went out drinking on weekends. They believed they were being responsible because they took turns being the

Karen Heckman and Ron Stark plot their future with two straws and a single soft drink. The outlook is for frugality.

Ron and I sharing a soft drink.
Photo from LHS Advocate *newspaper, spring 1961.*

designated driver who didn't drink on that particular night (and this was many decades before having a "designated driver" became fashionable and de rigeur). We all went over to Tony's house, and somehow Ron and I ended up in a separate room together. He was a little tipsy, and he laid his head in my lap, and we talked for hours.

Looking back on it, I don't know why I fell for Ron so quickly and completely. He certainly was unlike any of my previous boyfriends. He was someone else's boyfriend, and all at once he and I were talking and sharing secrets of our lives. I had always thought of Ron as a "bad boy;" he was sarcastic, with artistic talent, but not studious—he had a sort of starving artist mystique.

I was just the opposite; I was an "obey the rules and don't make waves" kind of girl; I loved learning and was looking forward to going to college. Ron had painted a mural on every wall in his bedroom, but he had no plans to pursue his artistic dreams or further his education. We were really opposites in many important ways that

I would learn later. I saw Ron as a James Dean or Sal Mineo character in the movie *Rebel Without a Cause*, and that seemed romantic.

Part of the reason I fell in love with Ron was because unconsciously I saw him as a "project;" I thought I could make him into what I wanted him to be. Another attractive attribute was the fact that my parents didn't think he was good enough for me. Well, that was a reason for me to prove them wrong. Besides, he had told me he loved me, and that was the first time any boy had said those three words to me.

Ron and I with two classmates at King's Drive-In. Photo from the LHS Advocate *newspaper, spring 1961.*

All these things combined to make Ron almost irresistible to me in my naiveté and innocence. We stayed together through the rest of our senior year in high school and we graduated from Lincoln High in June 1961.

My Twenties—What Comes Next?

Chapter

5

> "Relax. You will become an adult. You will figure out your career. You will find someone who loves you. You have a whole lifetime; time takes time. The only way to fail at life is to abstain."
> —Johanna De Silentio

I HAVE ALWAYS FELT THAT OUR TWENTIES should be about exploring the unknown and trying new things. Unfortunately, it took me twenty-three years and a major disruption in my life to understand what I should have learned in my twenties. Based on my own personal experience, I believe this is an important life lesson to understand and accept in your twenties:

You don't need to marry when you're twenty-one or decide the path of your life at this very minute.

Your twenties are a decade to try out new activities, new hairstyles, new jobs, new places, new partners; a time for you to discover your own personal right path for your life. It's a decade of learning, investigating and processing, not necessarily making those decisions that can affect the rest of your life.

In the 1960s, after high school, all my friends were either going to college or planning a wedding. I was engaged to my high school sweetheart, but still lived at home with my parents while I attended the University of Nebraska on the Betty Crocker scholarship I had won. I was excited about learning and was studying English. I enjoyed writing and toyed with the idea of some type of writing career or being an actress, doing something creative. I also began working at an insurance company while attending college.

I was concerned because my fiancé, Ron, did not attend college but went directly to work in a trade after high school. He didn't like the fact that I was going to college, meeting new people and having experiences which didn't involve him. Ron became threatened by the fact that I was pursuing my educational goals because they were a part of my life that was separate from him.

We never fought over these issues, because usually I didn't say much. I didn't like conflict and was unsure of myself. I thought I would never find anyone I would love as much as I loved Ron. But we were so young and hadn't experienced what it was like to live on our own and figure out how to take care of ourselves. In truth, I didn't know what love looked like or what to expect from someone who professed to love me. It took me many years to learn what love meant, and I didn't totally understand until I was in my forties.

But it was the 1960s, and I was just twenty years old, innocent and naïve, and engaged to be married. I have no recollection of the marriage proposal, or if it was simply assumed as the next step in our relationship. I mean it was either get married or break up in those days. So, I gave in to my fiancé's wishes and quit college in 1963 after two years. My parents were not at all happy about that.

Neither of them had attended college, and they wanted that experience for me. My folks wanted the best for me and felt they knew better than me what that was. That was probably true when I was twenty years old.

My dad repeatedly told me, "He's not good enough for you. You don't have the same goals."

I felt high expectations from my father. This can be a good thing if it helps children want to excel, right? But over the years I feared that I would let my father down— it was my job to exceed his expectations and make him proud of me. He liked to brag about many things in his life (including his children), and he often embellished his accomplishments. Sometimes it seemed we were only accessories for him to make himself look better.

My father always had to be right about every observation. If my brother or I learned something in school and discussed it with our father, if he didn't agree he would argue long and persuasively and could talk us out of what we had learned.

I also began to notice the interaction between my parents. I don't remember my mother having any opinions that weren't first proclaimed by my dad, and she always acquiesced to him. I don't ever remember her having an opinion of her own that differed from dad's. I don't know if my father had convinced her that he was always right and she stopped giving her own opinion, or if she just didn't want to fight about anything. Perhaps this is where I learned to "go along to get along," to be a people pleaser.

In the end, however, they did support me when I finally decided to get married. They paid for my wedding in 1964.

In the year before my wedding, however, I experienced one of the most traumatic and painful events of my life, along with the rest of our country. It was one of the determinant moments of my life.

November 22, 1963

It was a cold, late-autumn Friday in Nebraska. The wind was bone-chilling and blustery, the trees trembled and the sky was overcast and foreboding as if anticipating the grave event that was about to occur. The streets of Lincoln were unusually empty for a Friday afternoon, especially just one day before the traditional football game between rivals Nebraska and Oklahoma.

As I entered the elevator of a downtown office building, two somber-faced men and a young secretary in tears stood mutely. Not wanting to intrude on some private grief, I looked straight ahead. One of the men said to me, "Haven't you heard? They've shot the President!"

"Which president?" I replied, thinking he meant a president of one of the corporations located in the building.

"JFK," he replied, "Those bastards have shot him!"

Stunned into silence, I thought surely that couldn't be true. Just that morning pictures had shown John F. Kennedy arriving in Texas. No one noticed as I hurried into the office; the other secretaries were huddled around a radio, crying softly; my boss stared blankly, uncomprehending, at nothing in particular. Then the fateful news was announced on the radio: "The President of the United States has died of a massive head wound." It was 1:00 p.m. CST.

No one who experienced that day could forget what they were doing at that moment. Whatever the personal, individual reactions, in that instant in Dallas, Texas, the fabric of a nation had been irrevocably, violently torn apart, much like Humpty Dumpty after his fall. Once again, a single shot had changed history and altered the course of human events.

At 12:15 p.m. that day, Mrs. Heckman (my mother), a forty-three-year-old homemaker, arrived at her monthly bridge group. Amiable conversation centered on children, grandchildren and club activities.

At 12:20 p.m., Mr. Stevens, an accomplished businessman and civic leader, was on his way to a luncheon appointment, immersed in last-minute details for the big deal he was about to negotiate. He nonchalantly hummed along with the popular song on the radio, "Blue Velvet" by Bobby Vinton.

At 12:35 p.m., Miss Brown, a veteran sixth grade teacher in her last year before retirement, began the afternoon history lesson—a discussion of the assassination of President Abraham Lincoln, almost exactly one hundred years prior.

At 12:45 p.m., Mrs. Miller, eight months pregnant with her first child, left her apartment and walked down the hall to do a load of laundry in the washroom.

At 1:00 p.m., as if a magician had waved his magic wand, an eerie stillness descended over the city as all normal activity ceased. Cab drivers stopped their cabs and sat listening in disbelief. Brought together in unlikely alliance, groups of people—young and old, black and white, rich and poor—gathered in front of television sets on display in furniture stores, staring at the unfolding spectacle. Students put down their pencils. Phones went unanswered. Secretaries stopped typing. Cars stopped in the street. Everything came to a standstill. United as one in grief and dread, the nation waited for confirmation, hoping against hope that this horrible nightmare was merely a hoax.

Mrs. Heckman received a phone call from her daughter conveying the tragic news. The smile faded from her face, and she motioned to the hostess to turn on the TV. The bridge game was over. The group sat transfixed as the drama unfolded like a horror movie before their eyes.

Mr. Stevens continued to hum as the announcer on the radio broke in with an urgent news bulletin. As he pulled his car over to the side of the road, which already looked like a parking lot, silent unchecked tears rolled down his cheek.

Miss Brown listened as the school principal announced the tragedy to the staff and students. From her history lesson on Abraham Lincoln, she was immediately brought back to the present and another slain President. *How do I explain this insanity to children*, she wondered. She sat down and tried to compose herself before facing her students whose tear-stained and unbelieving faces looked to her for guidance and comfort.

Mrs. Miller heard the news from her landlady who ran into the hallway screaming incoherently. Rushing back to her apartment, Mrs. Miller was greeted by a frantic neighbor from Argentina who wanted the families to pack up and hide out in the country to escape the terrorists she assumed would now be roaming the streets.

Everywhere it was the same: tears shed unashamedly by those who never cried; angry voices raised in shock and disbelief; stunned silence because no words could suffice to describe the horror… the unbelievable horror.

President John F. Kennedy's assassination touched all of us; it changed each of us personally as it changed the fate of the nation and the world. I spent the next three days huddled at home with my brother and parents in front of our black and white TV watching the entire spectacle unfold before us. It was almost too much to accept, and no one knew how to react. No one spoke much. We had our meals when it was time to eat, but we ate in silence in front of the TV—something only done on rare and special occasions.

We, along with our Washington Street neighborhood, the town of Lincoln, the State of Nebraska, and the entire nation will never forget two-year-old John John saluting his father's casket, the black, riderless horse with boots turned backward, widow Jackie Kennedy along with Kennedy brothers Robert and Teddy walking behind the black artillery caisson pulled by six horses carrying the President's body—so many other images, each more poignant than the last.

John F. Kennedy was our American hero who had been struck down. What had the world come to? We all felt the randomness of the act, the immutability of it, and its effect on the future. If our President could so easily be brought down, no one was safe. This was a turning point; our lives and the world's future had been inextricably connected and changed forever. It is widely perceived that JFK had only begun to reach his peak; his best was yet to be, perhaps. Assassinated at forty-six, his potential was unfulfilled, his dreams never realized, his plans never completed.

Life Continues

In the face of death and horrendous loss, the universe continued spinning, and we went on with our lives. My wedding to Ron took place only six months later. Originally, Ron and I had planned to get married in the fall or winter of 1964. However, we moved up the date because of the Vietnam war and the draft. At that time, married men were not being drafted. So, by moving up the wedding date, we had hoped Ron would avoid the war. I really didn't think about whether that was a good idea or if we should just wait to see what might happen with the draft. Then, just a few months before the wedding, the Army began drafting married men. So in the end, moving up the date had not affected Ron's draft status, and shortly after our wedding day Ron joined the Nebraska National Guard.

I admit I acted precipitously in marrying when we moved up the wedding because of Ron's draft situation. That should have been the first warning sign that we married in haste and not for the right reasons.

I had been the "good girl" my whole life—that was my "role" and how I was brought up. So, I continued that role in my marriage. No one ever suggested to me that I should think about what I really wanted my life to be. I learned not to make waves, not to get angry, I didn't learn to think about what was really important to me. I never questioned moving up our wedding date because Ron had convinced me it was necessary. Marriage was just another step in the journey of life, normally occurring around age twenty-one. I simply accepted that "natural" progression without looking inward to figure out what I really wanted.

Ron and I were married on May 16, 1964, in First Plymouth Congregational Church. We were both just twenty-one years old. My four bridesmaids were high school friends, who wore long lavender dresses, and I carried a bouquet of lavender roses—something new at the time (lavender was my favorite color then and continues to be a favorite). My dress was simple with puffy flowered sleeves. I kept that wedding dress in a cedar chest until 2015 when I sold my house.

The wedding vows were the usual "love, honor and obey." It was not customary to write your own vows in those days. The reception for the afternoon wedding was

My wedding day, May 16, 1964.

in the church parlor with cake and ice cream—no dinner. An "after reception" party for close friends was held at my parents' home. The wedding gifts were all displayed in the dining room. My uncle opened champagne in the kitchen.

Ron and I left for our honeymoon directly from this party. I changed clothes upstairs in my childhood bedroom, and we drove away in Ron's car to spend the night in our apartment not too far away.

A second warning sign occurred that night when the air conditioning in our apartment suddenly broke down, and we did not consummate the marriage on our wedding night.

I was a virgin when I married. My mother never talked to me about what to expect in the marital bed. I was innocent, and it took me many years to be able to actually enjoy sexual intercourse. That's another reason for waiting to marry until you have had more life experiences and have gained more knowledge and common sense.

Ding, ding, ding...

Our honeymoon began the next morning. We were planning to go to Colorado, but only got as far as Kearney, Nebraska, when we decided we wanted to return home so we could open the rest of our wedding gifts.

Ding, ding, ding.

Married Life

The first years of our marriage were typical and I was happy. I didn't notice anything unusual, but perhaps that was because I only had my parents' marriage as an example.

I began working full time, and we settled into a marital routine in our small one-bedroom apartment in a four-plex on the corner of 25th and D Street. The average rent for such an apartment in the 1960s was about $120 per month. We bought furniture for the apartment, including a French provincial gold couch which, at the time, I thought was the epitome of fashion. A small dining area was in an alcove off the living room with the kitchen right beside.

Both of us had lived at home until our marriage, so we never discussed what it might be like living with someone who wasn't our parent and how to divide household duties after marriage. I simply fell into the routine of cooking dinner after working all day, doing the shopping, cleaning and laundry. And Ron quickly got used to that arrangement.

I won the Betty Crocker Homemaker of Tomorrow contest after all.

We had friends during the early part of our marriage, but didn't do many activities together as a couple. I played bridge with other married women friends. Ron bowled and continued to go out drinking with a group of his male friends. This quickly became a regular routine for Ron;

the only difference between his drinking when we were married and when he was in high school was that there was no designated driver anymore. He became less responsible about his drinking, although it was not yet out-of-control. I didn't understand fully that he might have a problem with alcohol, so I did not try to talk to him about why he drank so regularly.

Besides the drinking, Ron and I had many other areas of disagreement, and many more would come up in the future. One of our major differences was the fact that he wasn't sure if he wanted children at all, and I was anxious to be a mother after a few years of getting used to marriage. For this reason, I was on birth control for the first six years of our marriage. In the 1960s important issues like birth control and having children often weren't discussed prior to marriage. Before we wed, we had never talked about having children, our finances and spending habits, or saving for retirement. Many issues and questions that couples should discuss before marriage were left unspoken.

Another major issue, at least for me, was the fact that I wanted to return to college. However, I was afraid to bring it up because even in the 1960s we needed my salary to pay our bills. In fact, after a few years I made more money than my husband. That was another issue that we never discussed and which widened the divide in our separate views of marriage and relationships. I continued to bottle up my feelings when I got frustrated and learned not to criticize or complain. We both continued to walk blindfolded through our lives, never talking about the future or what was important to us.

Aesop said, "it is thrifty to prepare today for the wants of tomorrow." However, we did not plan and we did not

Our first home on South 41st Street, 1968.

save money. That is one of the biggest mistakes I made in my marriage, and something in later years that I have tried to instill in my grandchildren—the importance of saving. Every woman—in fact, every person—should have money of her/his own, for whatever they want, so no one person is dependent on someone else for money.

One goal on which my husband and I agreed was buying a house. Even though we had not saved for a down payment, we were lucky enough to know a builder and real estate agent who owned several small homes. He let us buy a small two-bedroom, one-bath home on South 41st Street using rent payments as our down payment. After two years of paying rent, we owned the house. We moved into that home in 1968. The cost was $15,000.

I did love that house. We worked on it, added a family room with a fireplace off the kitchen, and fixed up the basement. I planted a garden and loved to pick mulberries from the tree in our backyard. We got a Boston Terrier named Biff, the first dog I had ever owned, and he was our baby for three years. One of the best things that happened in that house was my pregnancy and the birth of our daughter, Jennifer. She was the best thing that resulted from my marriage.

The Birth of a Child

Ron and I had never talked about trying to get pregnant. In fact, this was the first time in our marriage that I had made my own decision without consulting anyone else. That was certainly out of character for me at that time. I just decided, after six years, that I was tired of taking birth control pills, so I just quit. I don't remember if I told Ron or if he discovered it when he found out I was pregnant. I figured it would take me about a year to get pregnant, but it only took three months. My husband didn't know how he felt about it, but he did accept the fact that he was going to be a father, and I definitely wanted a child. *Maybe*, I thought, *that would make me feel that I was on the right path for my life.*

When I think back to that time in the late 1960s, I still have questions that I can't answer being so long removed from the circumstances. When did things start to go wrong? Was it when I stood up for myself the first time when I decided not to take birth control anymore?

Ding, ding, ding...

I was working at an insurance company when I learned I was pregnant. I fainted at work with no warning, and had never fainted before or since. My coworker helped me into her office and had me lie down on her couch. She's the one

I loved being pregnant, 1971.

who said, "I think you might be pregnant." And the doctor confirmed it. (We did not have home pregnancy tests in 1970.) I was never sick once during my pregnancy. I could eat anything I wanted and do anything I wanted. I had absolutely no problems at all during the pregnancy. In fact, I had never felt so good as I did when I was pregnant.

I wrote a poem about the night Jenny was born.

The Night You Were Born

It begins slowly at first —
A cramp in the middle of my back,
I'm not even sure what it means.
Two hours later...
the pain migrates around my middle
and takes up residence just below my navel.

It's time, hurry up, to go to that
white antiseptic sterilized place where
everyone wears starched green uniforms
and plastic name tags.

Assigned to a bed with a curtain around it,
I'm poked, probed, shaved, shot with hypos.
Now I'm prepped and ready, so they tell me.

Relax, slow, breathe, go with the contraction,
that pain shooting through my innards
always back to front, never sideways.
Contract, breathe, relax, contract, breathe, relax,
Breathe breathe, inhale, exhale, don't stop now
push push bear down bear down...
Let it go... go... go... go
PushdownPushdownPush... Wait

A black mask snakes toward my face.
I struggle and fight to push it away.
Get away get away, not fair not right,
I've done all the work, suffered all the pain
Now denied the final triumph.
Can't fight anymore. Okay, I surrender.
Doctor knows best. Fade out; eyes close...

Eyes open. It's over. And I have my prize—
6 pounds, 3 ounces, 18 inches. A gorgeous baby girl.
And her name is Jennifer Leah.

With my baby daughter.

When I woke up, the doctor said I had a daughter, and he called her "Bright Eyes." My whole world changed the minute she was placed in my arms. No words can convey the feelings at that moment—joy, terror, apprehension, and total happiness.

It's difficult to explain, but all mothers will understand, how much a child changes your perspective and attitude about your life and what's important. Suddenly that new pair of shoes isn't as essential as a teddy bear or doll; that old car we have can make it a few more years. Nothing becomes as important as the health and well-being of your child. As Dante Alighieri said, "Three things remain with us from paradise: stars, flowers, and children."

And I must say, the first time my husband laid eyes on his daughter, he was a goner. He fell head over heels in love with her, and she could do no wrong.

The first seven years of Jennifer's life were spent in our little house on South 41st Street. It seemed like everything might be okay with our marriage, perhaps because we had

Jenny at two years old.

someone between us and in whom we could pour all our hopes and dreams. I was lucky to be able to go back to work when Jenny was six months old because my mother-in-law took care of her. I didn't feel quite as guilty since she was being cared for by a family member.

Shortly before our daughter was two years old, the decade of my twenties was finished. I entered my thirties unsure about the future and not knowing what it might bring or where to turn. I was still a new mother and didn't have the courage to figure out what I wanted and what was important to me. I felt like I couldn't take care of myself and my daughter on my own, and I felt I was responsible for the happiness and well-being of two people... so I just carried on, not thinking, merely putting one foot in front of the other.

How Did We Get Here?

It is said that we teach people how to treat us. So how did I teach Ron to treat me with verbal abuse and controlling behavior? How did I teach him to make fun of me, insult me, etc.? And why would I continue to subject myself to this kind of behavior for so long? Was it because I was trying to keep the family together for our daughter's sake? Was it because he had succeeded in making me feel responsible for his happiness?

Although I can't remember exactly when Ron's controlling behavior began (though I didn't understand what it was at first), I do remember that it started with small incidents like teasing and calling attention to my shortcomings, often in front of others. If we were talking politics, he might say, "You think you're so smart, but you don't know anything about politics." He also made statements that "lovingly" disparaged me in front of others. For example, "Just because you're in college doesn't make you smarter," or, "You may be in college, but a degree won't give you any common sense."

In the beginning, these remarks seemed like endearing light-hearted fun. I never was quick enough to think of a witty response to his sarcastic put down or joke at my expense. So I just laughed along with everyone else. But inside these degrading remarks accumulated in my mind like walking through a field of prickly nettles which stick to the skin and continue to cut, if you don't get rid of them.

My Thirties—Motherhood and Red Flags

Chapter 6

"Never allow waiting to become a habit. Live your dreams and take risks. Life is happening now."
—Paulo Coelho

MY THIRTIES BEGAN WHERE MY TWENTIES ended. It felt like I was just sleepwalking through life, anesthetized, waiting for something to happen to give me a clue as to what I should do. My thirties felt mostly like a time of "wait and see and figure out how to continue." It was like the calm before the storm. Nothing impactful or life-changing occurred, and I didn't have a lot of time for self-reflection and soul searching. I just followed the same path that I had begun in my twenties and tried not to think about the future. The year was 1973. I had been married for nine years. Jenny was two and a half years old.

As happy as this time was with my daughter, after a few years of working and mothering, I started to question some of the ways in which my husband expressed his love for me. Ron had been telling me since we were married, "I can't live without you." At the beginning, I thought that phrase was romantic. But as other controlling behaviors began to creep into our marriage, it slowly began to seep into my consciousness that maybe this statement was actually a form of control.

I also began to notice increased questioning about my actions—where I had been and what I had been doing. His statements and questions started to get inside my head, and thoughts started to grow that perhaps I was responsible for his happiness, in addition to my own. That is a great burden to put on the shoulders of another human being, especially someone you profess to love. But at the time I felt it was my responsibility, and the closed-in feeling (like being in prison) mushroomed in my soul.

At Work

I had begun work at the Water Center at the University of Nebraska-Lincoln (UNL) in the fall of 1971 when Jenny was six months old. I loved my secretarial job and everything I was learning. I had studied English for two years before I quit college, and I was learning accounting skills, office

management, how to write business letters and plan national conferences, as well as working on and editing professional articles with my boss. I was fortunate to have a boss who could see my potential and who encouraged me to expand my skills. After a few years, I was promoted to Administrative Assistant.

On the job (in a wig) at the Water Center at UNL, 1972.

My boss had high expectations and gave me tasks that I felt

unqualified to undertake. He expected more from me than I expected from myself.

For example, when I had been editing a conference proceedings, he called me into his "cubicle." He tried to give me advice and tell me that I could do a better job than indicated in my preliminary manuscript. He made suggestions that, in my eyes, implied that I wasn't up to this task.

This was the one and only time during my entire career that I was actually brought to tears by a supervisor's words, and I fled down the hall. Later he told me that he was only trying to encourage me by saying that I wasn't working up to my potential and that he believed I could be better.

It turned out to be the best lesson he could have taught me, and I continued to learn under his tutelage. My boss and mentor showed me that I was capable of growth, learning, and excelling in ways I never thought possible. His belief in my abilities helped improve my confidence in what I could accomplish, and I took on more and more projects.

At Home

Jenny started kindergarten in 1976. We were still living in our first home on South 41st Street near Calvert Elementary School. We walked her to school, and our neighbor picked her up after school with their same-age daughter. Their daughter, Kathryn, was rambunctious, inquisitive and unafraid, and I thought she might not be a good influence on Jenny. After a while we let the girls walk to school alone because it was only a few blocks with no busy streets. (I know that is something unheard of today, but times were more innocent then.) We had taught Jenny

Jenny at six years old.

not to talk to strangers or get in a car with anyone except her parents or grandparents.

One spring day while I was working, I got a phone call from the school. Two police officers had picked up Kathryn and Jenny, who had decided to skip school that day. They were picking flowers from other yards on their way to school. I don't know if someone called the police or if the police just happened to be near the school.

The officers saw the two girls, stopped them and asked, "Why aren't you in school?" The officers then offered to take the girls to school.

Jenny resisted and said to the officers, "I can't get in your car because my parents told me never to get in a car with someone I don't know."

I'll never understand how they finally persuaded her to get in their car, but it's a story I will never forget, and I'm sure she hasn't forgotten it either.

Another time, we left Jenny alone for one hour to go next door and visit with our neighbors. Jenny was about six years old; we were sure she was sound asleep, and we were only gone for a short time. However, when we returned, we found her sitting on the steps near the back door crying her eyes out because she had awakened from a bad dream and went looking for us to comfort her. She thought we had left without her. It broke my heart to think our actions made our daughter cry, and I felt like the worst parent in the world.

Jenny still teases me about that incident. Believe me, we learned our lesson and never again left her alone even for a few minutes until she was much older. If we did go out with friends, we always took her to one of her grandparents. We were lucky that both of our parents lived in town, and they took turns looking after Jenny whenever we needed a babysitter. We never had to hire a teenage babysitter for her.

Even though I was enjoying my job at UNL, and I thoroughly loved spending time with Jenny, my husband and I continued to grow apart. By the time Jenny was in school, Ron always insisted we do everything together as a family, all three of us, even if it was something that I wouldn't enjoy. I thought he and his daughter should have their own relationship, just the two of them, doing things together like bowling or playing softball.

Jenny and I had activities that we enjoyed together like reading, learning to ice skate, going to garage sales and dancing lessons. However, whenever Ron was involved in an activity with Jenny, I always had to be included, whether I wanted to or not. I believe it is important for a girl to have a relationship with her father who can teach her things that a mother can't, like how she should be treated by boys as she grows older. This was a subject of constant bickering between Ron and I, and it was never resolved.

While we continued to live our life day-to-day, never confronting our disagreements, I believe we were subconsciously trying to figure out a way to keep our marriage together for our daughter. We never really talked about the problems in our relationship, mainly because I didn't insist on it. I didn't like confrontation and had not yet learned to speak up for my beliefs and feelings. I had learned to shut my mouth and stuff my feelings and needs deep inside.

I simply suffered in silence, which is never a good idea.

A healthy relationship should always include a feeling of safety and being able to discuss whatever is bothering each party, without being judged. Because I didn't have a healthy relationship, I was faced with an increasingly persistent dilemma: What's more important—breaking up a family or being an authentic woman with her own feelings, ideas and thoughts?

Not knowing how to mend our relationship, we started talking about buying a bigger house—because nothing says you have a successful marriage like buying a new house. Real estate prices had greatly increased since we bought our little house in 1968. We finally made the decision in 1978, when I was thirty-five years old, and sold the little house on South 41st Street for three times what we had paid for it—$45,000. We bought a beautiful newly-built brick home in a newer south neighborhood just east and south of 70th and Pioneers Boulevard for $68,000. The house had a beautiful

Inside our new house with the big picture window, 1979.

large picture window facing south; there were no houses around, only farmers' fields.

From that picture window, I watched thunderstorms approach and was mesmerized by the vivid lightning strikes and loud thunder. In the fall, I watched the trees change color from green to orange, yellow and red. I also enjoyed lounging on the sofa in the winter while basking in the warm sunlight that passed unfiltered through that window. This huge window was one of my favorite features of the new home. We didn't have to cover it with curtains or blinds because no one could see in. That window in our new home was my front row seat to the changing moods of Mother Nature and the outside world beyond my own little cocoon of work and home.

We also put a lot of work into that split-level house. The downstairs was unfinished, so Ron spent time bricking in the fireplace and hearth and building a brick-faced bar. We had room for a piano in the basement, and I wanted Jenny to take piano lessons as I had done as a child. One of my greatest regrets is that I didn't continue with piano lessons as I grew older. I loved to sing and would have loved to play the piano while I sang.

After we had lived in the house for about three years, we decided to add an above-ground swimming pool in the large side yard. We thought it would be a good place for Jenny and her friends to hang out in the summer. Ron and his friends leveled the ground, installed the pool and built a deck around half of the pool. I also loved relaxing in the pool after work and on weekends.

As Jenny grew up, it proved to be a popular hangout for her friends, as well as for our friends and neighbors. That was one of the best investments in the house that we ever made. I do believe that Jenny had a good childhood in that beautiful home. At least, that was true for about the next six or seven years.

Friends and family enjoying our new swimming pool in the 1980s.

Jenny with Spike

Spike

Remember the summer you were six years old
and you caught a caterpillar in a mason jar,
you added a stick and some leaves to keep it alive
and you punched holes in the lid so it could breathe,
and then you sat and sat and watched it for hours?

Remember how surprised you were when the green
bumpy bug started spinning itself into a
mummy-like gray cocoon attached to that stick
and you asked, "How could it stay alive inside
and how could it eat?" and you kept it by your bed at night?

Remember how an orange-black butterfly emerged
covered with drops of wetness and bits of gray cocoon
clinging to its body, struggling to open its wings
which seemed stuck together like thin strips of Velcro,
and you exclaimed, "It's alive!"?

Remember how you opened the lid and the orange-black
Monarch flew up and landed on your left shoulder
and we could hardly see it because it matched your orange blouse,
and how still you stood as it explored your shoulder and
finally opened its wings like a prisoner flexing new-found freedom?

Remember how you christened him "Spike" and we all watched
him take off from your shoulder, and we chased him across
the field next to our house, and how he got smaller and smaller,
and finally was only an orange-black speck in the sky?

There's a mountain in Mexico
where these orange-black former prisoners gather in huge numbers.

I hope Spike found his way home...

Relationship Red Flags

Much as I loved our new home, I became increasingly dissatisfied with our relationship and unsure of the future. Ron and I continued with our two disparate views of our marriage. In fact, at times I began to feel as though I might actually be two different people: I was a confident, outgoing, intelligent woman in business and in public; while in private, as a wife and mother, I was meek, compliant, and subservient. My daughter never saw my public persona, only my private "home" self. She wasn't learning from me how a woman could have her own thoughts and feelings in a healthy relationship and that she could determine her own path in life.

The controlling behavior and incessant questioning grew more frequent. I perfected my skill of walking on eggshells, and didn't want to do anything to disturb the calm superficial surface of our existence. I was plagued by uncertainty, never knowing what might be a "trigger" for Ron's anger.

I had always felt an undercurrent of threatened violence bubbling just beneath the surface. Ron's anger was easily provoked and could erupt with the slightest provocation. No, he hadn't hit me so far, but he was very verbally abusive. When I would bring up an idea that he hadn't thought of, he would quickly smack it down, implying that I was stupid for thinking or discussing such an idea.

In those days, not much information was available (or I just didn't know it was available) about the destructiveness of verbal and emotional abuse and controlling behavior. I knew about physical abuse and spouse beating, but I still didn't realize or understand how relationships could be brought down by the insidious and silent destruction of verbal abuse. No one I knew talked about it or what might be done about it. So, for me, it was difficult to explain to others the damage that could be caused by verbal abuse. I felt like people would not understand and might think, "Well, it's only words; it's not physical."

As the years passed, however, I learned by living it that verbal abuse is a killer of one's self-image, and reduces to nothingness the joy and hope that continuously try to take root in the soul. Verbal abuse is like the "death from a thousand cuts"—a slow, lingering process of torture that is cumulative and constant. It slowly eroded my self-confidence and ability to believe my own thoughts and feelings.

As the end of my thirties approached in the early 1980s, I finally began to notice a number of what I called "relationship red flags." These warning flags included:

- drinking too much while staying out later on "boys' nights out"
- a longer list of taboo subjects that caused angry outbursts and verbal attacks
- becoming increasingly more threatened by my work and success
- keeping more secrets and talking less
- more frequent escalations of jealousy and controlling behavior

I didn't clearly recognize it at the time, but all these red flags popped up with increasing frequency as my thirties ended, and then became increasingly worse as I progressed into my forties.

Ever since high school, Ron had liked to drink. I always thought he was just a social drinker, and for a time this was true. However, as we grew older, he continued to go out with friends and his alcohol problem became worse. A pattern was established. After he went out drinking, he would come home drunk and angry and yell at me for whatever offense he thought I had committed. Then he would sleep it off, go to work and be contrite the next day, apologizing and asking for forgiveness. He was always so sweet the second day that I would give in. However, he would continue to berate me for causing his problems, never taking responsibility for his actions.

I didn't know what to do to help my husband. I was afraid and didn't speak up for myself. The norm for me was being yelled at and then accepting Ron's apologies and feeling that whatever was wrong was probably my fault.

Ron could never talk to me and admit that he had a problem with alcohol, and I was afraid to broach the subject of addiction. I believe he was self-medicating because he was depressed and didn't know how to talk about it. I also came to believe that Ron was jealous of my success and accomplishments at work and in other areas of my life. He was unhappy in his job at a print shop, not satisfied with how his life was going, and I believe he felt like the only thing he could control in his life was me. Unfortunately, I didn't know how to change the situation or even bring up the subject.

Ron's controlling behavior was also worsening. He increasingly would question me when I got home after being at work or somewhere else without him. As my job responsibilities continued to grow at the Water Center at UNL, my marriage continued to deteriorate. I had begun traveling infrequently to conferences with my boss. The Water Center also sponsored many national conferences at the University, and I was in charge of all arrangements. This meant longer hours and spending days away from home when I was out of town. Then when I returned home, I faced a barrage of questions and accusations about exactly where I had been and what I did. Ron continued to accuse me of enjoying my job more than I enjoyed being at home.

He used certain statements and words to make me question my self-worth and intelligence. And I never felt strong enough to defend myself. Here are some of the phrases I heard more frequently about ordinary, everyday, common situations:

"Why did you turn there? I told you it's faster to go this other way."

"How could you say something so stupid?"

"Where were you and why weren't you home?"

"Why are you wearing that outfit? I told you it makes you look fat."

Other various "fill-in-the-blank" statements were commonplace in our conversations:

"Why didn't you do _____ instead of _____?"

*"Did you forget
that I asked you
to do _____?"*

*"Don't you remember that I don't like
it when you _____?"*

He continued certain well-used tactics to control me with words; each sounded loving, but were actually like chains around my soul, keeping me in bondage to his wants and needs:

"I can't live without you."

"Don't you know that I will always love you?"

"You're the only one who can help me."

He did agree once to go to counseling with me after we had moved into our new home, but he wouldn't accept a female counselor. He always felt our male therapist was agreeing with him, and therefore, was convinced that whatever was wrong was my fault. The most telling sign that the counselor was not the best fit for us was during a separate session he said, "You have a Cinderella complex. You don't worry about tomorrow because you always assume that something or someone will come along and rescue you." And he was probably right.

The decade of my thirties seemed to plod along day after day with nothing changing in my personal life. I mostly denied or refused to think about our problems, while accepting that I couldn't change anything, or simply wasn't brave enough to. So, I existed, I worked harder and longer at my job and found satisfaction in that arena and elsewhere.

Jenny was almost a teenager at twelve years old. My feelings of unrest and uncertainty were growing stronger day by day. It seemed like I was constantly searching for something to make me feel better, something that could fill the emptiness deep inside me.

Part III

You Can't Make an Omelet Without Breaking Eggs

"New beginnings are often disguised as painful endings."
—Lau Tzu

My Late Forties—Turning Over a New Leaf

Chapter

7

"You start dying slowly if you do not change your life when you are not satisfied with your job, your love, or your surroundings."
—Pablo Neruda

AFTER VERBAL ABUSE, DIVORCE, BANKRUPTCY and selling our home, I wondered, *What comes next; what now?*

It was late 1988. I was alone, relying only on myself for future decisions about my life's journey. It was a liberating yet daunting feeling. I could no longer blame any mistakes or difficulties I might encounter on any other person. My future would be entirely of my own making... wait a minute... *my future would be entirely of my own making.* That had been my goal all along, during my tribulations and missteps. I had finally made it. I could do anything, be anything I wanted to be. I could go anywhere I wanted. I didn't have to ask permission of anyone for what I wanted.

That was one of the most exhilarating and terrifying revelations I have ever had in my life. My entire life was right there in my own hands, in front of my eyes—all I had to do was take the first step, make the first decision about where I wanted to go in my future.

I felt liberated to finally be able to be who I was—a positive, confident woman who wanted new adventures and to continue learning and to write.

[Note: As I was writing the paragraph above on May 23, 2016, Hannah Huston, an elementary school teacher from Nebraska was singing her original song on *The Voice* called "I Call the Shots." She sang, "I now know what I want, and now I call the shots."

I couldn't believe it when I heard her singing. I had to run right back to my computer and add this paragraph to this chapter in my life's story. That song described precisely my feeling after my divorce. It was like that song was talking about my own journey over twenty-five years ago. Serendipity, coincidence, or a sign telling me that I had followed (or am following) the path chosen for me? As Albert Einstein once said, "Coincidence is God's way of remaining anonymous."]

Now it was time for a new beginning—just me and my daughter. After our house was sold, we moved into an apartment at Capitol Beach Lake, and we lived there for a year and a half. It was a new and scary experience for me— it was the first time I had chosen my dwelling by myself. It was fun being close to Capitol Beach Lake. Our apartment was really just one big open space with the living room, dining room and kitchen all together. I never liked having the kitchen open to the living room. I always had to keep the kitchen clean because everyone could see it.

But my past wasn't quite finished with me yet. Ron continued to call me. Sometimes I wouldn't answer the phone if I thought he was calling. (Again, this was before cell phones.) I always knew that it was probably him calling when he wouldn't leave a message. Other times I would talk to him because I was still concerned about his mental health. I tried but was unsuccessful in getting him to see a therapist who might be able to help him.

How was I finally able to resist Ron's pleas to come back and help him even after we were no longer together? Because I knew I could no longer help him; he needed professional help both with his drinking and his depression. And I realized that he was continuing to try to control me to get what he wanted. Because it had worked for so many years (saying that he couldn't live without me), perhaps he thought that same tactic might work again, or maybe he just didn't know what else to do. He didn't seem to be able to move or concentrate on what he needed to do for himself.

Ron's brother and his wife were wonderful friends to me during the separation, divorce, the whole sordid mess. They were kind and understanding and they never blamed me. They understood Ron's problems with depression and

Jenny and me after her high school graduation, 1989.

alcohol and tried to get him help. I was always thankful for their consideration and understanding during this turbulent upheaval.

Jenny graduated from high school in 1989 while we were living in the apartment. She went to her senior prom in a simple pink dress that my Mom made for her. She looked so beautiful that night, and I was so happy that my troubled marriage and divorce hadn't stopped her from living her own life. During this time Jenny was undergoing some of her own emotional soul-searching.

"What's bothering you?" I asked quietly one evening. "Can I help you with something?"

She then asked me one of the most important questions a daughter could ever ask her mother: "How do you know when you're in love?"

Wow, that sure had me searching for answers. We talked about the question for a long time. As we talked, I gave her my definition (though perhaps flawed because of my circumstances) of what it means to be in love. As I talked I was also seeing a poem develop in my mind.

At that time, I was putting together a graduation album for Jenny with pictures and poems from every stage of her life. This was one of the most important poems I've ever written for any occasion.

Letting Go

I tiptoe into your bedroom, sit down cross-legged
on the floor and watch you sleep
because you're growing up and I'm not ready to let go.
Your long dark hair unfolds behind your head
like a casually discarded Oriental fan.
Your right arm curls around a faded pink teddy bear,
clinging to something you still understand.
Moaning softly in sleep, you turn and give
the teddy bear a hug as if to say
you're not quite ready to let go.
Just yesterday you asked me how to tell when you're in love —
as you search the eager faces of every boy who
shows an interest, not sure of what you're looking for.
Fumbling for the words, I turned away.
It's important that you understand and I may
never get another chance.
How do you explain that you can give your heart
without losing yourself;
That the seed of love begins with friendship
and blossoms into a union of hearts, minds, and souls;
That love means acceptance—but not surrender.
I think of all this as I watch you sleep
and know that it will happen much too soon.
Someday you'll put away your teddy bear
to sleep in the arms of a stranger.
And then I'll say goodbye and let you go.

Jenny made a decision about her future. She broke up with her former boyfriend and began dating the man who would eventually become her husband a few years later. She also enrolled at the University of Nebraska-Lincoln in architecture in the fall of 1989. I'm not sure that's even what she wanted to do, but I believe she thought it would make me happy.

The first house I bought all by myself.

A New Home

By the time I was forty-seven years old in 1990, Jenny and I had grown close. I don't believe I would have gotten through my forties without my daughter by my side. Even though I had been through a bankruptcy, I could still qualify to buy a house—because you couldn't declare another bankruptcy again for, I believe, seven years. So, we decided to begin looking for a house with separate spaces for the two of us. We spent quite a while looking with an agent, and finally after some months, in the late spring of that year, we found a perfect house for us. It was right next to South 41st Street but in a different neighborhood (further north) than our first home on South 41st Street.

We moved into the home on July 1, 1990, and I lived there for the next twenty-five years of my life. There was an apartment in the lower level that Jenny could have as her own living space.

In steps Marv.

A New Relationship

Another momentous change in my life had been progressing slowly during all this turmoil. I had known Marv for many years. Then we began working together at the Conservation and Survey Division at UNL. He supported me through all my marriage and divorce chaos. He gave me time off whenever I needed it, and we became close friends. I highly recommend looking to good friends if you're considering the possibility of a life partner. We began actually dating sometime in 1990, so that year I had a new home and a new "significant other" in my life.

Since we were both "older" when we began dating, we've never quite known how to refer to each other. "Significant Other" is such a mouthful, and yet boyfriend and girlfriend seemed so juvenile. So, we

Marv and I at a wedding in 1997.

never really defined our relationship; we just accepted what was. He was and continues to be the kindest, most generous and accommodating man I've ever known. We made room for each other in our separate lives. Neither of us had a desire to marry again. I had never before lived on my own, and I found that I really enjoyed it. I am a Pisces after all, and we enjoy other people in small groups, but need to recharge our batteries with a regular amount of alone time for thought and reflection.

So, Marv and I began our relationship living apart yet being a couple, and we continued on the same path, separate yet together. In the years to come we would spend part of each year traveling together to various parts of the U.S.

I was ready to move on to the next stage of my life. And it was a good thing because those next three years of 1991, 1992 and 1993 were three of the busiest years of my life.

1991—High School Memories

I agreed to act as chair of the Reunion Committee for the Lincoln High School class of 1961's thirtieth reunion, which meant planning all the reunion arrangements and activities. Of course, the reunion planning began just after we moved into our new home a year before. Anyone who has ever been involved with the organization and planning of a big event like this knows how much time and how many decisions are involved. We had probably twenty-five people on the planning committee, and we met every month. The reunion was scheduled for July 1991.

The reunion theme was "The Pearl Anniversary." We had been out of high school for thirty years, and (as noted in the reunion yearbook), we asked the question "What does this make us?"

- Rapidly approaching the big five-0
- Some of us grandparents
- Some of us wearing bifocals
- Some of us counting calories, cholesterol, blood pressure, etc.
- Some of us referring to our periodontist, podiatrist and proctologist by their first names

The reunion was successful with a great turnout. After all the planning and meetings too numerous to count, I had a wonderful time, and as chair, I received the gift of an "L" pin on a bracelet. It was a high school tradition that athletes who earned letters in a sport would "pin" their girlfriends, i.e., give them their "L" pin. In high school, the boys I dated were not athletes, so I never got an "L" pin. I loved getting this gift at our thirtieth reunion and I still have that bracelet to this day.

LHS Class of 1961 at their Thirtieth Reunion.

To my surprise, Ron showed up at the reunion. He was still drinking heavily and he often would come around to the new home Jenny and I were in, but during the reunion he behaved himself and there were no problems.

A New Business

Somewhere in this time frame I attempted to return to my first love—writing. I had heard of a type of business where writers performed a service to clients by writing poems to celebrate special occasions like birthdays, weddings and anniversaries, and thought that would be a great business. I had always loved writing poems. Maybe I could make some extra money.

I advertised in the newspaper, put up flyers and told everyone I could think of about my new business called "Personal Verses." I printed the verses I created on beautiful paper to make them special for the recipient, then framed the poem and delivered it personally, if requested. The most difficult part of the business was knowing how much to charge. I finally decided to charge by the number of stanzas in the poem.

The business didn't last long because I was so involved in other activities, but I enjoyed it immensely. It seemed to make clients happy and was a unique kind of gift. And, most importantly, I was returning once again to my life's passion, my first love—writing.

1992—A Wedding Celebration

Another reason I was so busy at the end of my fifth decade was the fact that my daughter and her boyfriend, Curtis, had decided to get married. They got engaged and moved in together in mid-1991, so we had about one year to plan the wedding. No, I wasn't happy that they moved in together (in my basement apartment), but Jenny was almost twenty-one and engaged, so it was her decision how to conduct her private life. I was just so happy to be able to focus on a joyous and momentous occasion for a change, and I threw myself wholeheartedly into the preparations.

Jenn and I had a wonderful year together planning her wedding. I didn't have much money, but her dad did help out financially. Her wedding dress cost about $500, which was a lot of money in 1992. The wedding was at Curtis's church (First Lutheran) on South 70th Street, with the reception and buffet in the basement of the American Legion Club on O Street.

The wedding was memorable for many reasons:

- First, it rained early that morning, and we were worried. But I said that rain on the wedding day was a good omen, and it did clear up in the afternoon.

*Ron and I with our daughter,
son-in-law, and our mothers.*

*My daughter's wedding,
July 11, 1992.*

- My greatest joy on that day was when Jenn asked both me and her dad to walk her down the aisle; I was so thrilled to be included in that tradition after all we had been through together.
- The beautiful and moving marriage ceremony when the couple declared their love and commitment to each other.
- Jenn and Curtis acted as ushers, greeting guests as they were led out of their pews (I had never seen that before at a wedding), and the photographer took a picture of all the guests as they exited.
- The horse drawn carriage ride from the church to the reception stopped traffic.
- The toasts and the traditions like the bridal bouquet toss (don't know who caught it) and garter toss.
- The couple's special song by Bryan Adams, "Everything I Do, I Do It for You," and their beautiful first dance made me cry.

- And finally, their departure at the end of a glorious day, as they drove off in their car decorated with cans tied to the bumper and signs.

I was emotional and teary-eyed that day. I'm sure all mothers have these same feelings on their child's wedding day. My little girl was all grown up and on her own. She had her own life to live, her own decisions to make, and her own life path to follow. I wrote her a letter on her wedding day trying to explain how much I loved her and admired her and wanted her to be happy. My only wishes for her were that she be happy and that we continue to be close friends as well as mother and daughter.

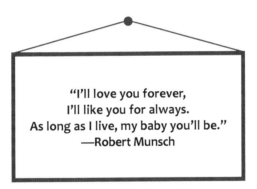

"I'll love you forever,
I'll like you for always.
As long as I live, my baby you'll be."
—Robert Munsch

My Fifties—
Celebrating My *Self*

Chapter

8

"You're never too old to set another goal or dream another dream."
—C.S. Lewis

MY FORTIES HAD ENDED ON A JOYOUS occasion—my daughter's wedding. And I started my fifties in my own style—by throwing myself a fiftieth birthday party in my new home of almost three years. I asked everyone to bring me fifty of "something" to celebrate. I got fifty pennies, fifty cigarettes (I still smoked in my fifties), fifty Q-tips, fifty pieces of candy, to name just a few. It was a great party, and I felt wonderful because I had wanted to celebrate, and I didn't wait for anyone else to throw me a party. I celebrated my "self."

My fiftieth birthday celebration.

Where my forties had been a decade of upheaval, turbulence and changes, it looked like my fifties might be a decade of growth, exploration and returning to my original path for my life. That didn't quite happen during this decade; however, I did start on the path of self-discovery and exploration. I tried new things, and learned to trust that whatever came into my life was for a particular reason, even if I might not understand it at the time.

As I entered into this new decade, I continued to work at the Conservation and Survey Division at the University of Nebraska-Lincoln. I really liked my job and all the people I worked with. After getting settled in my new home and getting past my daughter's wedding, I was ready for a less hectic schedule. However, in my fiftieth year, I had another big celebration to help plan—the 100th anniversary of the Conservation and Survey Division. Although the organization was established in state statute in 1921, it had actually been in existence since 1893. We were planning a big remembrance and party for all past and present employees and the many public servants the Division interacted with.

Displays of project activity lined the hallways of our offices on the first floor of Nebraska Hall. Speakers talked about the history of the Division and its many contributions to improve public perceptions about the natural resources of Nebraska. We had set up displays of antique equipment as well as newly-invented futuristic technology to improve our understanding of the state's natural resources. Along with my daughter's wedding, this celebration also had taken well over a year to plan and execute.

Public Speaking

Being newly independent, and the kind of person who likes to be involved in a project of some sort, I decided to rekindle my interest in public speaking. Unlike most people who would say that speaking in front of a crowd is one of their biggest fears, public speaking has never frightened me—as long as I have a plan or a specific duty to execute.

I am somewhat of an introvert, someone who detests cocktail parties that involve speaking with strangers on the usual inane subjects, but someone who enjoys having deep, heart-to-heart conversations about the really important things in life with a few close friends. I have always enjoyed public speaking because it gives me a part to play when I am involved with a large group of people.

I checked around for various Toastmaster groups in Lincoln to see if there would be one that was convenient for me to attend. Many met early in the morning, and I am not an early morning person. I also noticed (and thought it was unusual) that there was no such group or club on campus; it seemed that would be a natural forum for an educational experience like public speaking. So, I decided I would get involved and start a campus Toastmasters group over the noon hour.

I did some research on how to get a group started and spoke to people in other groups as well as gathering together a group of people who, like me, were interested in this kind of activity. The group received permission to begin a campus Toastmasters group, and we were the charter members. We held our meetings on East Campus so we named the group E.C. Speakers. I remained a member for five years and got my five-year pin. I just loved writing and giving speeches on many different topics. I learned so many lessons about public speaking from everyone in that group. And to my surprise and delight, that group is still going strong today. I am proud of my accomplishment in starting that new campus group.

Giving Back

In the early 1990s I wanted to find other ways of contributing and helping other women who might be faced with an abusive situation similar to my own. I decided to find a volunteer activity and chose R/SACC (Rape/Spouse Abuse Crisis Center), which in 2007, changed its name to Voices of Hope. Their goal is to empower those who have experienced relationship violence, sexual assault and abuse. Their mission is to provide crisis intervention, twenty-four-hour advocacy and case management services to victims of domestic violence, sexual assault, incest, stalking and related forms of abuse.

I was trained to answer the twenty-four-hour hotline where victims could call for help and information. I worked in that position for over two years. Listening to women tell their stories and understanding what they felt was a rewarding experience, while at the same time sad and stressful. Some of the stories I heard were heart-breaking and harrowing. I was always worried that I might not be able to help someone in a serious predicament, or that I would give them incorrect information on how they could get help. I carried those intense conversations with me for many months afterward.

When I felt I could no longer handle being a crisis line volunteer, I changed my focus to volunteering at Friendship Home, a shelter for abused women and children. Friendship Home supports, shelters and advocates for victims of domestic violence and their children. They provide a continuum of safe, confidential shelter options—from emergency shelter through transitional housing. They also provide crisis intervention services, case management and emotional support to those being sheltered, helping them to rebuild their lives, free from fear.

These two volunteer activities were essential to my growth and understanding of my own past abusive situation. I learned how to help others while at the same time learning to heal my own soul. Any woman who finds herself in an abusive situation and feels all alone and helpless should look for these wonderful caring organizations in her own town. Don't be afraid to ask for help when you need it.

> Voices of Hope (in Lincoln, Nebraska): 402-476-2110
>
> Friendship Home: 402-437-9302
>
> National Domestic Violence hotline: 1-800-799-SAFE (7233) and 1-800-787-3224 (TTD)

1994—A Sad Ending

The first year of my fifties was filled with many accomplishments and looking ahead to my future. The next year was one of sadness and looking back.

After our daughter's wedding, I didn't see much of Ron, but it seemed that his depression and drinking were getting worse. I often talked with Ron's brother and his wife about helping Ron get into some kind of support group. Ron wouldn't listen to them either when they tried to convince him to see a psychiatrist. Finally, his brother began investigating the possibility of going to court to have Ron declared incompetent so he could be institutionalized and get the psychological and medical help he needed to recover. Sadly, that never did happen.

Ron still called me and sometimes stopped at my new home to talk to me. Unfortunately, his ideas had not changed even after the divorce. He continued to tell me that I was the only one who could help him. I reminded him that I was not a professional counselor, and I didn't have the expertise to give him what he needed. One morning in early 1994, there was a knock on my door. I looked at the clock, and it was almost 2:00 a.m. I knew who it had to be. I was so angry. I rushed to the door.

"What do you want now?" I said tiredly.

Ron replied, "Can I just come in and talk for a while?"

"It's the middle of the night, and I have to work tomorrow. This simply can't continue. There is nothing I can do to help you. I am not qualified. You need to see a professional and leave me out of your life," I said, shutting the door.

But of course, then I couldn't go back to sleep. My mind was churning with all kinds of scenarios about what might happen. I began to feel guilty that I wouldn't talk to Ron. But I also knew that we both had to move forward, which meant away from each other. We had been divorced for about five years. I didn't know how to get him to accept responsibility for his actions and to get the help he needed. Yet, I still was concerned about him because we did have a daughter who needed both of us.

Several weeks later I got a phone call at work from Ron's brother.

He said simply, "Ron committed suicide last night." He died on February 17, 1994.

The words hung in the air like wispy clouds, and it seemed I could actually see them written on my office wall. The world suddenly seemed to slow down and quit turning. I was speechless, literally unable to open my mouth and utter words.

He went on to explain, "A friend found him in his car with the motor running."

All I thought about was our daughter. How could I ever tell her what had happened? How could I find the words to explain it to her? How would she understand it? And would she blame me?

This was a scenario that I never thought about during my sleep-deprived ramblings. And then the guilt again whacked me in the head full force. If only I had talked to him that night when he came over. If only I had tried harder to convince him to get help. If only I had stayed with him... If only... If only. Those are two of the saddest words and the most useless phrases in the English language.

No one can predict the future. No one person is responsible for the actions taken by another person. But those are just empty words when one is faced with the unthinkable, the unexplainable, the unbelievable as I was that day.

Above all else, the overwhelming emotion I felt was one of immense sadness at this willful taking of a life. Ron would miss so many wonderful highlights of his life to come, especially his grandchildren. But I couldn't spend time wondering why; I had a mission to perform. I had to leave work and go tell my daughter.

It was the middle of the day when I drove to Curtis and Jenn's apartment, as slowly as I possibly could while I tried to form words into sentences in my head about what I would say. When I arrived, I sat in the car for a few quiet moments of reflection and prayer, asking God to give me the words to speak, the emotions to understand and the wisdom to help my daughter.

Jenn was expecting me; I had called to ask if I could come over to talk. I slowly climbed the stairs, trying to retain my composure so I wouldn't dissolve in tears when I saw her. This was the hardest thing I had ever done in my life. I knocked on their door. I went inside where they were both sitting with expectant, inquisitive looks on their faces. Without even thinking I simply blurted out, "Jenny, your dad is gone. He committed suicide last night."

Then I rushed to embrace her and broke down sobbing; I hadn't cried until that moment, until I held my daughter in my arms, hoping to provide comfort, but actually feeling comforted by her in that awful moment. We cried together, and then Curtis hugged his wife tightly.

As we planned Ron's funeral and put his favorite objects with him in his casket (a pipe, a statue of a Boston terrier, which had been our family pet, a replica of his revered Jaguar sports car), Jenn and I drew even closer. I spent many hours contemplating what went wrong, why I had taken one road after the marriage was over and Ron had taken this final path.

I wondered why our marriage had collapsed and why we couldn't find a way to talk to each other. I could suggest many possible answers, but I truly didn't know why this had happened. I had more questions than answers: about the marriage, about the effects of depression and alcoholism on a relationship and especially about suicide. Were any of these outcomes preventable? Did all of these sad aspects of my life (alcoholism, depression, divorce, bankruptcy and suicide) happen for a reason—que será será, what will be, will be? And if so, what might that reason be?

I couldn't answer those questions then and still can't. All I knew was that it was up to me to live my best life, to be the best person that I could be, to help others who might face similar situations, and to make something positive come out of all this suffering and sadness.

I also found it difficult to understand what drove a person to suicide. I wanted to understand, but I didn't know if it was possible to truly

> If you are suffering from depression or contemplating suicide, PLEASE KNOW THERE ARE ALTERNATIVES AND THERE IS HELP AVAILABLE. Call the National Suicide Prevention Lifeline 1-800-273-TALK (1-800-273-8255).

comprehend depression unless you've been there yourself. After Ron died, a friend talked to me about suicide and depression. She explained, "Suicide is never about wanting to die or trying to hurt those left behind. Suicide is simply an attempt to stop the horrible pain a person is suffering."

As is so often true for life in general, after all these tragedies, the next two years would be two of the happiest of my life.

The Joy of Being a Grandparent

Thank goodness, after that tragic interlude, my life seemed to turn around. In that same year of 1994 at a family Thanksgiving dinner, my daughter told me that she was pregnant. We were all overjoyed that after such tragedy just nine months prior, we had a great joy coming into our lives. Curtis and Jenn weren't going to find out the sex of the baby; they wanted to be surprised.

Something strange and inexplicable happened during that announcement. After Curtis and Jenn had left, on my kitchen counter I found a small gold replica of an angel, like an embossed decal that you might stick onto a piece of paper. I had nothing like it in my house, and I asked my daughter if she had brought any craft supplies with her (which she hadn't), so I couldn't explain where this mysterious "angel" figure had come from. I kept the decal and taped it to my refrigerator. Because I believe that angels exist on earth and coincidences are often God's way of getting our attention, I chose to believe that this was placed in my home for a reason—that my grandchild would be an angel in my life. I have kept that little decal for over twenty years and I still look at it every day to remember the wonderful news it represented.

The pregnancy passed mostly uneventfully. Both grandmas helped paint the baby's bedroom, and we all got to leave our handprints dipped in paint on the wall. Then we also got to choose the name we wanted our grandchild to call us and sign our handprint. I chose "Nana" and Curtis's mom chose "Granny." The time spent getting ready for the new family addition was so special, and I felt lucky to be so involved with the joyous event.

Our grandson, Anthony Trevin, was born in the early morning hours of Monday, July 24, 1995. I won't go into more detail about his birth, because that is part of my daughter and her husband's life story. The most beautiful moment was when Curtis came out of the delivery room and announced to the waiting grandparents: "I have a son." Tears of joy were rolling down his cheeks, and soon we were all crying. Such a joyous moment. I was now officially "Nana" at fifty-two years of age!

I soon came to realize the truth of an old Irish blessing: "Children are the rainbow of life, grandchildren are the pot of gold." Being a grandparent had all the joys of parenting and none of the responsibilities. And we could spoil the grandchildren to our heart's content. Happily,

My grandson, Anthony.   *My granddaughter, Elizabeth.*

our joy was expanded just seventeen months later, Friday, December 20, 1996, when my granddaughter, Elizabeth Haley, was born.

I got to be an integral part of their lives, picking them up at noon from kindergarten each day and taking turns babysitting with Granny and Pa. So many happy family holidays were spent together throughout the years.

I hold fond memories of the many activities we attended as the grandkids grew—Anthony's baseball games from the time he was five years old, and Elizabeth's soccer and softball games. I believe that if you are involved in helping to raise your grandkids through their early years, in most cases you will be lucky enough to maintain a close relationship for the rest of your life. So far, this has been true for me, and my family will always remain at the center of my life.

What I Know For Sure

As my life continued to expand and I had new adventures, I also learned important life lessons—things I know FOR SURE.

Parents will always love their children more than children (after they grow-up) love their parents.

And this is as it should be. This is the way of the world as it was from the beginning. Your children are moving forward and must focus on their future. That doesn't mean children don't love their parents; it's just that parental love will never be the focus of their lives, especially after grandchildren are born. As we age, however, and at least in my opinion, we continue to focus on our children, and if we're lucky our grandchildren; we want the very best life for them and will do almost anything to help them on their life journey. As noted in *The Lion King*, that's just the "circle of life."

World Travels

In October 1993, Marv and I took our first extended, scrapbook-worthy trip together. I had always wanted to see New England in the fall, and that was our goal on this vacation. I named it the "Three-M vacation"—Montreal, Maine and Massachusetts. We drove up into Canada to Montreal, and I got to try out my French there with the French-speaking Canadians. We spent five days in that beautiful city.

We then drove on to Maine, one of my favorite places in the United States. We stayed in Bar Harbor on Mt. Desert

Island along the rocky, rugged East Atlantic coast. The Bar Harbor Inn was quaint and charming, just what I expected in New England. The foliage was gorgeous, and we watched the sun rise over Cadillac Mountain in Acadia National Park, which is the highest point along the North Atlantic seaboard and the first place to view sunrise in the U.S. from early October to early March.

After five days at Bar Harbor, we drove on to Boston where Marv was attending a geologic convention, and we met friends there. We toured the sights of Boston, with its many historical sites and monuments. After the conference ended, we drove home. It was a wonderful two weeks, and I always learned so much on our road trips.

I still would rather take driving vacations than flying, because I get to just enjoy the beautiful scenery wherever we travel in this diverse country of ours. I have always liked exploring out-of-the-way highways and by-ways and the many small towns along the way. Small-town cafés (no matter what state we might be traveling through) are one of my favorite dining experiences. The food in these local cafés is unique to the region, inexpensive, and some of the best food you will find anywhere. I highly recommend trying small-town cafés with home cooking whenever you get the chance.

The Dalai Lama once said, "Once a year, go someplace you've never been before." Marv and I took many major road trips throughout my fifties. We traveled to forty-five of the fifty states, all glorious, educational and inspirational trips. Some of my favorite trips are listed below:

- Our three-M Vacation to Montreal, Maine and Massachusetts in 1993

- Oregon, Seattle and Victoria, British Columbia, in the fall of 1994
- Boston, Massachusetts, and Martha's Vineyard in the summer of 1997
- Albuquerque and Santa Fe, New Mexico, in December of 1997
- North and South Carolina in 1998
- Jackson Hole, Wyoming, and Yellowstone National Park in 1999
- Las Vegas, Grand Canyon and Bryce and Zion National Parks in 2000
- New Orleans Jazz Festival in 2002 (this became one of my favorite destinations)

The year after my second grandchild was born, I had my first experience as a world traveler. I love to travel, and that year I had a special treat in store—Paris—one of the items on my bucket list.

Marv was attending a conference in connection with his work in Nebraska on low-level radioactive waste disposal. A world-wide conference was being held near Troyes, France, and he asked me to go along. Having never been overseas, I had to get a passport. We were planning to attend the conference and then drive to Paris to spend a week sightseeing.

I wanted to experience April in Paris, so there would be no travel agency planning for me. I planned our whole Paris adventure specifically to our own interests and tastes—a truly authentic Parisian holiday.

I wanted to plan this trip so we could design it to fit our own personal wishes. Two of my goals for this trip were to stay in an authentic local French hotel (not an American chain hotel) and to stay near the center of Paris on the Seine River so we could walk to many popular sites. I also purchased a French-English dictionary so I could practice my French before the trip.

April in Paris, 1997.

Though we did have computers at work in the 1990s, their use was generally limited to scientific research and work-related purposes. I wasn't on the internet yet, so I went to a bookstore and bought actual books to find the information I needed to plan our trip to Paris. Frommer's and Fodor's Travel Guides were the preferred sources for travelers. It was in these books that I found great facts about hotels in Paris, how to get around, places to eat, popular tourist sites, etc.

In planning this trip I took into account all I had learned from planning numerous successful national conferences at UNL, as well as every travel adventure I had ever had (both good and bad). All these past experiences, along with the travel books, helped to guide me in the right direction for planning the trip of a lifetime. I listened to my inner voice that too often I had ignored in the past, and I heard "go for it, you can do it," so I did—and the trip was a resounding success.

I certainly didn't want to stay in an American hotel in Paris; I searched for a typical local Parisian hotel. I investigated many possibilities and finally settled on the Hotel du Quai Voltaire, a charming, small (thirty-three rooms) family-run hotel on the west bank of the Seine River right across from the Louvre Museum and the Tuileries Gardens. The hotel dated from the nineteenth century and has had such distinguished guests as Charles Baudelaire, Richard Wagner and Oscar Wilde, among many others.

I loved that charming little French hotel on the Seine. The hosts were the owners who spoke limited English. I had taken two years of French in college, and wanted to try speaking French as much as possible. We got by quite nicely. I had heard rumors that the French people were not very friendly to Americans. I certainly didn't find that to be true. I felt they appreciated my trying to speak their native language, and they could usually understand what I was trying to convey.

The elevator in the hotel was only big enough for two or three people with luggage, but we didn't care. When we left our hotel we usually took the steps down (105 steps) instead of the elevator.

I have always been enamored with the "City of Lights," and it certainly did not disappoint. Paris was quaint, clean and easy to walk through. I was walking where the ex-patriot writers of the 1920s like Hemingway and Gertrude Stein had trod. I had read Hemingway's *A Movable Feast* before the trip, and felt as Hemingway said in that novel: "If you are lucky enough to have lived in Paris as a young man, then wherever you go for the rest of your life, it stays with you, for Paris is a moveable feast."

The view from our room took my breath away, although the room was small by American standards—about twelve by twelve feet, with a separate bathroom. But I didn't even notice because the windows of the room were almost floor to ceiling covered by lace curtains, like most of the French windows in all the small towns we passed through on the ride to Paris. And most French windows also had no screens; they were often left wide open. We never had a problem with bugs inside. Another difference between American and local French hotels was that there were no washcloths in the bathrooms. I'm not sure why that even mattered, but I loved wondering.

After a long day sightseeing, we would lie in bed at night facing the huge windows (which we left open) and listen to the sounds of the river: the water lapping against the concrete embankments, the Batobusses (tourist river taxis) which cruised up and down the river day and night, and the bright lights from these boats that would shine up into our room as they passed (as if the guide were telling the riders about our hotel).

I kept a scrapbook and running commentary of our five days in Paris, and it still gives me such joy to look at the pictures and relive our European holiday—the one I dreamed up, the one I planned, the one I actually experienced. There was no internet, I had never heard of a travel agent, I just did it all myself at the library. I decided the world was my oyster and there were many pearls I wanted to discover.

Of course, we saw all the usual sights of the city (on our own schedule) including:

- The Champs-Élysées, one of the most famous boulevards in the world, with trees lining both sides of the street, bikers and skaters, flowers and fountains and crowds of tourists.

- The Arc de Triomphe, constructed in 1806 by Napoleon to honor the French patriots who fought and died in the French Revolutionary and Napoleonic wars.
- The Eiffel Tower, a wrought iron lattice tower named after engineer Gustave Eiffel whose company designed and built the tower. It was constructed as the entrance to the 1889 World's Fair. It is now the most-visited paid monument in the world and is 1,063 feet tall, about the same height as an eighty-one-story building. We ascended to the first level of the tower, but I was too afraid to go any higher. Even so, the 360-degree view of the entire city of Paris was magnificent.
- The famous couture fashion houses on the Rue du Faubourg Saint-Honoré, including Christian Dior, Versace, Valentino and many others.
- The Élysée Palace, the official residence of the President of the French Republic since 1948, which contains the office of the President and the meeting place of the Council of Ministers. We passed by this residence during one of our walking tours, and I happened to be out of film (in the "old days," you had to actually put film into a camera to take pictures), so I sat down on the step of a building to change rolls. A lady gendarme came running over to me speaking French rapidly.

"Je ne comprends pas," I said (meaning I don't understand).

"Anglais?" she replied, and I said "Oui."

She then explained in English that I couldn't sit there because it was the Élysée Palace, and the

President was inside working. In other words, this was like the White House or Capitol Building right in the middle of an ordinary looking Paris street. Needless to say, we got up and quickly walked away. But we did come back on the other

Élysée Palace in Paris where I got into trouble.

side of the street to take pictures. That was quite an adventure!

- The Louvre Museum, of course—a beautiful museum located right across the bridge from our hotel. We walked and walked and walked. We saw many wonderful paintings and statues, and we could take pictures of any of them—including the Mona Lisa! This really surprised me. In my scrapbook is a ticket which said 45 Francs to enter the museum.

Other notable sights we visited included Notre-Dame Cathedral, Place de la Concorde, Sacre-Cœur Cathedral in the Montmartre region (which is located atop the only mountain in the area of Paris), Place de Tertre (also in the Montmartre region), which was jammed with street artists painting and drawing, and the magnificent Tuileries Gardens.

Another of my favorite Paris places was Les Deux Magots, a cafe frequented by the painters and writers in the 1920s, where you could sit outside at a table and drink a glass of wine and just watch people go by.

Near Notre Dame Cathedral in Paris, April 1997.

We also crossed many bridges from the Right Bank to the Left Bank of the Seine and back again. My favorite bridge was Pont des Arts, one of only five pedestrian bridges that crossed over the Seine. On this bridge musicians played and sang, lovers kissed, and we watched the sunset on our last day in Paris.

With all of the changes in my life, the challenges, and upheavals, bridges hold a metaphorical and literal message of connection, progress, and overcoming obstacles. I seek out bridges in my travels because they change the lives of the people living there.

What I Know For Sure

Never procrastinate or put off expressing your feelings.

As Alexandra Potter wrote: "Don't ever put off telling someone how you feel about them, don't assume that they know, because they might not and it might be too late." I have certainly learned over the years not to put things off, especially telling people how much they mean to me. Never, ever put off telling someone "I love you" for a week, a day or even a minute. No one can foretell the future, and if you don't say it now, you may never get the chance.

In January of 1997, my brother almost died after

having suffered a totally unexpected and unexplained stroke at a young age. That was a wake-up call for me, like the heel of someone's hand hit me on the side my head. Thank the Lord, he pulled through and is fine today with only a few physical limitations. Ever since that day, I don't hang up the phone after talking with a family member without saying, "I love you," even if it's just, "Love ya." For me, those words are never trite, will never grow old, and cannot be said too often.

That reminds me of a precious memory. My mother always would stand at the door and wave to my brother or me and watch us drive out of sight when we left her house. Somewhat annoyed, my brother asked her once why she did that. Her answer also changed his attitude about expressing love. She told him "If you would leave and something would happen to you, I would always regret never fully having said goodbye to you and watching you leave until I couldn't see you any longer."

Although actually saying the words "I love you" is important in relationships, I only recently accepted the truth of another important life lesson—that there are other ways to show love besides speaking or writing about it, although those are my preferred ways to express feelings and emotions. But I now fully understand that others (especially of the male variety) can show love without words. It has taken me many years to accept this truism in my life.

My love, Marv, is not a wordsmith in expressing emotions, but he does so many things that show me he cares. For example, he really listens to what I say. I once casually remarked to him that my walking shoes were getting really old and I needed to buy some new shoes. He had originally given me my New Balance shoes years ago by redeeming some of his credit card points. A couple weeks later when I went to his house for dinner, he silently handed me a box. Yes, you guessed it; the box contained a new pair of the exact same New Balance shoes. Now to me that says love (and I know he will be embarrassed that I am sharing this story). He does so many other things like that—knowing what I need before I even mention anything.

I continually remind myself that just because someone doesn't say the words doesn't mean that they don't feel the emotion. However, just because your partner may express love differently, don't let that keep you from shouting your love with words or actions, whatever is right for you. I have learned to finally accept my need to verbally express my feelings and I do so with quotes, cards and words as often as I can.

New Church

In my mid-fifties, I began to exercise more to control my weight and stay healthy. When I wasn't working, I would walk all around the Randolph neighborhood in various directions, exploring as I went. I enjoyed seeing unique styles of homes and gardens in the area. On one of these walks, I discovered a small neighborhood church about six blocks from my home.

I felt drawn to this little church and stopped in to visit the next Sunday, and the next, and the next, no longer hearing the self-doubt and insecurity that I was not worthy. I felt called to this particular church, but for what reason, I didn't know. Soon I had found another extended family—a family of faith. I formally joined the congregation in 1998. It was here that I found Jesus again, or rather Jesus found me, and I welcomed Him back into my life. I now believe that the reason I was led to this church was to learn a particular lesson of faith and acceptance. It was at this small church that I learned an important spiritual lesson—I finally understood that I had been saved by God's grace alone, and that I didn't have to do anything special to deserve His grace. I simply had to accept it and then try to lead a life that exemplified God's love.

I joined the church choir, served on various committees and twice was elected as an elder to serve on the ruling body of the church. I also acted as liturgist, often reading scriptures during the worship service, and on occasion when our pastor was gone, I would speak about the bible verse of the day. I enjoyed my association with the church and all the church members, and continued as a member of this church for seventeen years.

Retirement from Full-time Work

The next important step in my life's journey occurred in 2000 when I retired from full-time work at UNL. I wanted to help my daughter and her husband who were building a house. I also used some of my retirement savings to redecorate my home. That was over a one-year project searching for just the right furniture and accessories. I had never before used an interior decorator because I never thought I could afford or deserved that luxury. Believe me, it was worth it for the discounts I received on all materials, but also the guidance and the validation of ideas and desires for my living space. The end result was beautiful and very French country, just like I had envisioned. My newly redecorated home provided another fifteen years of happiness.

I came to realize that retirement money I spent for the redecorating would probably have been lost in the following year because of the stock market decline after the horrific attack on the United States on September 11, 2001.

9/11/2001

For me, this was the second of those once-in-a-lifetime occasions when people know exactly where they were and what they were doing when a life-altering event occurred. The first of those dates was November 22, 1963, the assassination of President John F. Kennedy. The second was September 11, 2001, when the entire world was changed once again—and again, not for the better.

I had begun working part-time for the School of Natural Resources at UNL and had a great deal of leeway in the hours I worked. On that clear, sunny, late summer day, I got up and showered, and then turned on the TV. Applying my make-up, I heard words in the background about a plane that had flown into the north tower of the World Trade Center (WTC) in New York. The on-air news anchors were trying to figure out how an accident such as that could have occurred.

I went over and stood in front of my bedroom TV to better hear what they were saying. Along with millions of Americans, I watched as tragedy unfolded. From the left side of the TV picture what looked like a big passenger airplane came into view and immediately flew into the south tower of WTC. It was 8:03 a.m. central time. A huge fireball erupted like a volcano, spewing smoke, steel and every kind of object straight up into the air. These objects then rained down like falling meteors on the surrounding area and all the people frantically trying to run away to some kind of safety. I stood transfixed—stunned, unbelieving, and yet knowing this was no accident.

I couldn't turn my eyes away from the horrible scene and the voices of terrified and emotional announcers who were watching and seeing people jump to their deaths to escape the fire. They tried not to show scenes like this, but I saw falling objects and knew those were people jumping. The horror of these scenes remains indescribable.

About thirty minutes later, it was reported that United Flight 77 had just struck the Pentagon. And another half-hour after that Flight 93 went down in Somerset County, Pennsylvania. In less than two hours, four hijacked planes had attacked the United States of America, and nothing would ever be the same again.

I hurried to finish dressing and drove to work—where no one was working. I didn't want to be alone in my grief and sorrow. Extreme patriotism welled up inside of me. Everyone around me was huddled together in front of two or three TV screens scattered around the office complex. Tears were shed, voices shouted in anger, and people argued about what was happening.

We all later learned the details of this first attack on our homeland since Pearl Harbor. Al Qaeda terrorists aboard three hijacked passenger planes had carried out coordinated suicide attacks against the World Trade Center in New York City and the Pentagon in Washington, D.C., killing everyone on board the planes and nearly three thousand people on the ground. A fourth plane crashed into a Pennsylvania field, killing all on board, after passengers and crew attempted to wrest control from the hijackers. The phrase of the day after that was Todd Beamer's "Let's roll!"

The business of living seemed to stop for days on end. People went about their business, but it was eerie. No planes overhead for days. People were connected to their TVs or radios and watched or talked about nothing else for weeks. More information was shared. We watched heroic rescues and many scenes of sorrow and death and funerals. Citizens from age five to ninety-five were affected, and the rest of their lives were irrevocably changed by the actions of a few mad men.

In another year and a half, I would be sixty years old. And for those eighteen months, nothing else really mattered to me except learning all I could about these heinous suicide terrorist attacks that had been unleashed against innocents in America. Who could make sense of this occurrence? Why had it happened? Again, so many questions, with no answers to be found.

And so, it was in this dark, gloomy mood of despair that seemed to grip the entire world, my sixth decade ended as I turned sixty in 2003.

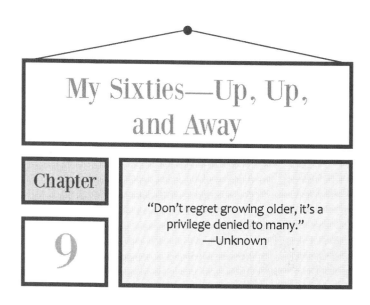

My Sixties—Up, Up, and Away

Chapter

9

"Don't regret growing older, it's a privilege denied to many."
—Unknown

THE YEAR WAS 2003. I TURNED SIXTY years old on March 18. I was determined this would be my decade of exploration and expansion of my goals and experiences. And I had added to my personal bucket list, which included:

- Spend as much time as possible with grandchildren
- Start another business of my own
- More volunteer work
- Hot air balloon ride
- Elephant safari in Africa
- Spend time at the beach
- Write my life's story

Hot Air Balloon Ride

The first item I checked off the list as a present for my sixtieth birthday (and my first new exploration into unknown territory) was the hot air balloon ride. That's all I wanted for my birthday. So, through the kindness of our families (because it is quite expensive), Marv and I got a hot air balloon ride.

Throughout my life, I had always been interested in hot air balloons—the dream of floating over the land untethered, the extraordinary beauty of a balloon against the sunset, and the images from old movies and exotic lands. Nebraska has a club of pilots and crews which I joined when I was in my fifties. For a time, I acted as a spotter and recorder during balloon races in central Nebraska. We noted the time that each balloonist would drop a bag on a target and note those that missed the mark. Then we would get in cars and race off to the next drop spot and do the same thing. I had such a good time during the couple of years that I helped with balloon races; however, I never got the opportunity to actually go for a ride myself.

No more, I decided. It was time for me to cross this wish off of my bucket list. Balloon rides only take place at sunrise or around sunset because of the wind restrictions.

Hot air balloon ride between Lincoln and Omaha, 2003.

Champagne toast after first hot air balloon ride.

We chose a sunrise ride on a chilly April morning. We left from an open field near Linoma Beach, a location on Highway 6 between Lincoln and Omaha, Nebraska. Jenn, the grandkids and my brother, Tom, would follow the balloon in a chase car.

We all stood around as the balloon was inflated with heated air which glowed in the darkness just before dawn. We even walked inside the balloon as it was filling up. Rich Jaworski of Euphoria Balloons in Omaha was the pilot. As the red and white (appropriate for Nebraska) balloon filled with air, I began to get a little apprehensive. The balloon soon was filled and upright, and we had to clumsily climb over the high wicker basket which was the passenger compartment and where the pilot skillfully guided the balloon. It's more difficult than you would think to climb into that wicker basket.

Then the pilot, Marv and I flew east toward the sun and the growing light of the day—up, up, and away. We flew over the Platte River and saw wild turkeys, deer and other critters. It was absolutely breathtaking and one of the most exciting adventures I'd ever had in my life. I felt exhilarated and free, unleashed from gravity and flying up into the sky.

At one point the pilot said, "You wanna have some fun?"

Of course, I answered, "Yes, please."

So, as we flew along the river, he dipped the balloon down toward a water-filled sand and gravel pit and actually dragged the basket in the water so that our feet got wet. I was afraid we would crash right there. But he soon took us straight up higher into the air again. The flight lasted just over an hour.

Now it was time to land. The pilot had to find an open space to put the balloon down. The chase crew and family had followed along as closely as they could on back roads. Air was slowly let out of the balloon, and we glided downward. This is the most difficult part of a balloon flight. No electric wires were in the area, but farm houses and fields dotted the landscape. We were heading straight for one such farmer's field. We just had to clear the fence, up and over we went, and then we skidded a ways along the ground

High over the Platte River as the sun rises.

and landed in a farmer's back yard. His wife and family came out to greet us. Of course, there was champagne for our first balloon ride. Marv and I had to get on our knees and pick up a plastic cup filled with champagne using only our mouths because according to tradition, that's what one does on their inaugural flight. But we managed it. Hot air balloon ride—check.

Balloonist's Prayer

The winds have welcomed you with softness.
The sun has blessed you with his warm hands.
You have flown so high and so well that
God has joined you in your laughter and set you gently
Back again into the loving arms of Mother Earth.
—Unknown

New Business Venture

I've always believed that it's never too late to begin a new activity, or to try something you've never had the courage to try before. My seventh decade was such a time for me. I still didn't feel old or limited by anything in my life. I was grateful for my health and mobility and wanted to take advantage of my good fortune, because no one knows what the future may bring.

In 2004, I felt I wanted to start a new business, but in an area I'd never thought of before. My daughter and I had always been close, and after some discussion, we thought we might try to start a cooperative venture. We weren't sure what kind of business because Jenn didn't want to leave her job as a daycare provider, and I was still working part-time. I happened to see a newspaper article (back then I still

ASAP
Errand
Service

Let us "lighten" your load

Anywhere errand

Service

Anytime

Personal shopping

No job too big or too small!

My daughter and I started our Errand Service business in 2004.

read the newspaper) on concierge or errand services in the bigger cities. These types of companies help busy people do some of the personal mundane chores in their lives, such as grocery shopping, dry cleaning pick-up and delivery, waiting at their home for service appointments and vacation services.

After a great deal of research, we decided on the name ASAP Errand Services. I bought a used van for the business, we printed brochures, business cards and developed a fee schedule. We were ready to go. Our motto was "Let us run while you have fun." We contacted businesses to see if they wanted to contract for our services to help take care of some of their employee's chores. We developed a list of clientele who used our services and began doing deliveries directly for some businesses like florists and stationery stores. We were even featured in a local newspaper article about this new type of personal service or concierge business. It was an exciting year for my daughter and me.

Jenn and I continued to work together, and the business grew in a year.

Family Move

Since my German grandparents on both sides had settled in Lincoln, Nebraska, after immigrating from Russia, no one in my immediate family had ever moved away from Lincoln. So, I couldn't believe what was about to happen to my little branch of the family tree. It felt like my daughter's branch of our family (with her husband and two children) was being sawed off and torn from the base of the tree.

I was lucky enough to have my grandkids around for the first ten years for Anthony and eight years for Elizabeth. When my daughter told us they would be moving to North Carolina, I thought, *I can't do this.*

I had no experience on how to remain close to a family who lived 1200 miles away. I didn't know how one goes about coping with this situation. I had grown up with grandparents on both sides who still lived in the same city as their children. My dad had one sister and one brother, and both of them remained and raised their families in Lincoln. My mom had two sisters and four brothers. Every one of them also raised their families in Lincoln. Some of the third generation of our German-from-Russia family (my cousins) had moved away from Lincoln to continue their life's journey, but no one on my particular branch.

Curtis worked for Goodyear Tire and Rubber Company which had a big factory in Lincoln. However, after working there for about ten years, the company was going to lay off employees during a business downturn. Some employees were given the choice of transferring to another Goodyear plant in other parts of the country. Curtis and Jenn decided that Curtis would transfer to the plant in Danville, Virginia. It was devastating news to me. I was heartbroken and couldn't believe I would be left here without my family.

When they told me, I jokingly told my daughter, "You and Curtis could just move and leave the grandkids with me here in Lincoln."

Anthony was going to be ten years old and Elizabeth was eight. They loved Maxey elementary school and had, in fact, built a house on the street right behind the school. The grandkids didn't want to move. But the decision had been made. After checking out the school situation, Curtis and Jenn decided to move to a small town named Eden, North Carolina. So, Curtis moved to North Carolina in March to check out the housing situation, and Jenn and the kids stayed to finish out the school year.

Because Jenn and I had gotten through some tragic situations already, we both felt we could live through this change; there simply was no choice, and this was one of life's moments that only feels tragic if you choose to look at it that way. After Curtis left, we spent lots of time together going to garage sales every Saturday, attending concerts together, packing boxes to be moved and getting their house ready for sale. I practically lived at their house; I wanted to spend as much time as possible with them. I had never been separated from my family before, and I didn't know what to expect or how I would get through this seismic shift in our family dynamic.

During this upheaval in our family situation, I had also been having some digestive issues. After a number of tests, it was discovered that my gall bladder was not functioning well and would have to be removed. So, I thought I'd be smart and schedule my out-patient surgery for June 5, 2005, the exact date the family would be leaving Lincoln. My thinking was that this surgery schedule would give me something else to concentrate all my energies around, instead of only being sad about the family leaving.

I will never forget our last night together, before my surgery and their trip across the country. Curtis had returned home some days before, and those last couple of days were spent loading up the rental truck with their belongings and a final cleaning of the house they had built. Everything I touched to move to the truck brought back precious memories of their life here in Lincoln—report cards, school tests and homework, drawings and handmade birthday cards.

My daughter is a "keeper"—she keeps almost everything that her kids did from their school days. Some of these memories were packed up in plastic containers, which I stored in my garage.

That last evening before the move, it began to rain, a gentle, constant shower with no lightning or thunder, as if God felt my heartbreak and was crying for me as well. I have always loved the rain and was never afraid to get wet. I believe that you're never too old to dance in the rain. So, I asked Anthony and Elizabeth to come with me to dance in the rain. We ran outside in our bare feet and danced and splashed and jumped in the puddles along the curb in front of their house. I wanted our final memory before they moved to be a joyous one, and it was. That is how I'd like to be remembered—dancing in the rain while my tears flowed freely.

The next morning, they were up before dawn driving to their new home, and I was having gall bladder surgery. Both journeys were successful. My family settled in Eden and continued along their life paths with my grandkids. The surgery helped my digestive problems, and the recovery lasted for a few days so I didn't focus so intensely on my daughter's and grandkids' departure. However, I missed the possibility of being able to see my family on the spur of the moment—calling them up and saying "Come over for dinner tonight" or going to kids' ball games and performances. It took me quite a while to get used to this new cross-country style of family interaction.

However, there was one positive development as a result of their move to North Carolina—they lived in the middle of the state, only FOUR hours from the beach. So, it was my plan to visit every summer and spend family vacations at the beach, which we did for the most part. My favorite beach in North Carolina was Wrightsville Beach near Wilmington. We rented a vacation house for a week and had wonderful times together at the seashore for several summers. The grandkids learned to boogie board and body surf. It scared me to watch them sometimes walk out so far on a large sand bar and to jump over incoming waves.

I wasn't quite as adventurous. I was perfectly content to bring my beach chair right down to the edge of the ocean and sit there with a large hat on my head and feel the waves come in and cover my feet and sometimes splash up my legs. I could sit there for hours daydreaming, laughing, and playing. I also spent lots of time walking on the beach in the early morning and again at sunset. I searched for and collected many kinds of sea shells. I still have these ocean mementos with me today in a large old-fashioned pickle jar. These times resulted in happy family memories filled with wonder, salt air and the ocean's roar. For me, there is nothing to compare with being at the confluence of sand and sea—it's where I will always want to be, especially with the people I love.

Sitting by the sea.

Our family at Wrightsville Beach, North Carolina, 2009.

What I Know For Sure

The most important blessings are the people in my life.

This is true especially for my daughter and two grandkids with whom I continue to have a close and nurturing relationship. When my daughter and family lived in the same town as I did, I was lucky enough to help take care of my grandkids over the first years of their lives. We were able to build a firm foundation of unconditional love, trust, support and acceptance. Because of this foundation, my relationships with my grandchildren, now that they are young adults, has continued to be very close and is one of the greatest joys of my life. And I am so blessed that my daughter continues to be my best friend, even though we no longer live in the same city.

I am also grateful for my close friends, both those who have known me for many years as well as those who have only recently come into or returned to my life. These friends bring me joy, laughter, understanding and support when I need it. I've learned that it's not the number of acquaintances we have that's important as we grow older. What is crucial to my health and well-being are the few close friends who I know I can always count on, who will be there when I need someone to listen to me and really hear me, and who will support me in whatever choices I may make.

New Writing Project

After a few years of racking up airline miles visiting the family in the summer and sometimes in the fall or at Christmas, I grew more accustomed to our long-distance life style. I missed them like crazy, and sometimes I would visit simply to see Anthony play baseball or see Elizabeth act in a play. But it was time for me to return to thinking about what my future might hold and where I might go from here. It was difficult for me living alone in a big house, but I was managing.

Then in 2007 (partly because I had originally worked at the Water Center for about fifteen years and was totally familiar with its mission), I was asked to take on a project for the School of Natural Resources, writing a *History of the UNL Water Center from 1964 to 2008.* Water has always been an integral part of Nebraska's economy and well-being in a state that depends on an adequate supply for all uses, including agricultural, industrial, recreational and wildlife habitat. The report highlighted the Water Center's many contributions to Nebraska and the nation regarding water resources. Not only has water been a source of joy replenishment and contentment for me, but now I had the opportunity to mix my love of writing with my fascination with water.

I worked with the former directors of the Water Center in writing sidebars for the report about their individual perspectives of the Water Center when they had been in charge. I had worked for three of the six directors over the years, and it was a joy for me to reconnect with old colleagues and work with them on this project. I researched the past in the UNL archives, wrote many pages of copy, obtained appropriate pictures and worked closely with an editor to bring this project together. It turned out to be a successful academic publication, and I was extremely proud to have been the major writer. It had been satisfying to again dust off my writing skills, and it gave me the feeling that maybe I had become what I had always wanted to be.

Retirement Eligibility

As I was finishing the writing project in 2008, I also turned sixty-five and was eligible for Medicare, so I no longer had to worry so much about paying for health care. *Well*, I thought to myself, *you're now officially "old."* Everyone wants to put you "on the shelf," because you're in a certain age category called "retirement." When one reaches this lofty age, it seems others have a certain view of how they (retirees) are expected live their lives in their "golden years."

However, I certainly didn't feel sixty-five, and I didn't know how to react to having reached this advanced age. I didn't want to retire. I was not ready at all. I liked being active, learning new skills, exploring new horizons, and continuing to expand my little corner of the world. It had taken a ton of work, and a lot of years to find my "self," and I was in no way ready to put my feet up and stop being productive. Besides, I still needed the money I earned from part-time work—that's a big incentive to continue working!

And I knew many other oldsters who had continued to work. One such lady in Nebraska was Sally Gordon. She had worked as an assistant sergeant-at-arms in the State Capitol Building, as well as a court reporter, model and state worker for numerous Nebraska governors for eighty-five years. In 2011, at the age of 101, she was honored as one of two of America's Outstanding Oldest Workers. She is one of my role models for aging with grace and confidence. Sally died on Valentine's Day, 2012, at the age of 103.

Having decided that I wasn't ready to retire, I looked around for my next earning and learning opportunity. I found it in an entirely new field that I had never worked in before—the fire department.

No, I didn't become a fire fighter. But I did work with many of them and other support staff at Lincoln Fire and Rescue; as the name implies, Lincoln Fire and Rescue is a combination fire/emergency medical services department. I began in the fall of 2008 and continued in this part-time position until finally retiring at the end of 2015.

I worked in the EMS billing department and was involved in reviewing all reports that the fire fighters were required to submit whenever they were called out on a medical response call. It was a rewarding job that I enjoyed very much. Those years sped by quickly and for the most part uneventfully. I worked, traveled to visit family and with Marv, took care of my house, enjoyed time with friends, and didn't really think any more about a writing career during this second half of my sixties.

A Life-Changing Year: How I Quit Smoking

In 2011 when I was sixty-eight years old, I accomplished something I had tried and failed to do many times during my life—to become a non-smoker. I never used the remedies they sold to help one quit smoking nor visited a hypnotist. I often quit for a few weeks probably once a year in the past ten to fifteen years. But for some reason, I just couldn't remain "a former smoker." Perhaps I just hadn't cared enough in the past.

It was winter, and I had a terrible cold and cough. In the past, I would often stop smoking when sick, but never thought I'd quit forever. I can't explain what was different this time. Maybe it was my age and thinking about my mortality. I had often heard of well-known people, like ABC newscaster Peter Jennings, who had quit smoking many years prior and then later developed lung cancer and died. Maybe I wanted to quit simply to remain a part of my grandkids' lives, to see what they might accomplish as they grew into young adults.

Front left to right: Karen, Curtis, Jenn
Back: my grandkids, Anthony and Elizabeth

Fighting a cold in 2011, I simply decided that if I hadn't smoked in five days and had made it through without much stress, why, oh why, would I ever start again? The toughest part of quitting was over—now all I had to do was change my habits. I had never been a heavy smoker—never more than one-half pack per day. There were places where I never smoked, and I never missed smoking when I was in those places—like my car, Mom's house, church, work, etc. And smokers had been banished from most establishments and had to go outside to smoke which was really no fun at all, especially during the winter.

So, I just quit. Or rather, I decided not to begin smoking again after recovering from my cold. Honestly, it was just a snap decision and I stuck to it. For some reason, it wasn't even very hard for me. I had an unopened pack of cigarettes which I put in the freezer, and my opened pack, about half empty, I crushed up and threw in the garbage. I did it! I really did it all on my own! It is one of the accomplishments I'm most proud of in my life. And I haven't been tempted to pick up a cigarette in these past five years.

I eventually threw away the full pack that I had stashed in the freezer after six months. I don't even know the current price of a pack of cigarettes, but I'm sure I have saved a lot of money by quitting. I don't think about it anymore. It's more unusual for me to see someone who actually smokes these days. My hope and prayer is that I didn't wait too long to make this momentous decision to improve my health and possible longevity.

My Mom Dies

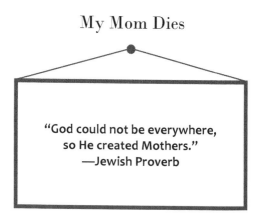

"God could not be everywhere,
so He created Mothers."
—Jewish Proverb

The biggest life-changing event of 2011 was the death of my beloved Mom, just twelve hours before her ninety-first birthday on September 22. Mom had been living alone in my dad's childhood home since he had died on December 15, 1993. I had always been close to my mother, but not particularly close to my father. In fact, I was always closer to the maternal side of my family than my paternal side.

My dad's death really didn't have a profound effect on my life, other than the fact that I had to teach my Mom many things about taking care of herself. She didn't know how to write a check; she didn't know about their bank account; she didn't know that Dad had no savings or life insurance. She was pretty much left to fend for herself, and I had to help her learn all these ordinary facts of life.

Mom had taken care of my father since he contracted Parkinson's disease about twelve years before his death. He became increasingly incapacitated which meant she had to do more and more for him. During the last few years of dad's life, she had to feed him and bathe him. That took a huge toll on Mom's health and well-being.

Although she missed my dad, Mom had actually learned to enjoy her new solitary life. She was active in Eastern Star and a Red Hat Club and had many friends. She loved to garden and always took good care of her little home. My dad drove a huge, old Cadillac, which Mom absolutely hated. So, she sold it and bought my little Mitsubishi from me (for $1), which she continued to drive until about three years before her death. Mom was short, and she continued to shrink as she aged, due to osteoporosis. I used to laugh at seeing her behind the wheel as she looked like a small child driving that car. But she loved her independence.

In 2006, after Jenn and her two great-grandchildren had moved to North Carolina, I was able to take Mom to visit them. She really enjoyed that trip, and it was the last time she traveled away from home. As Mom grew older, and her bones grew weaker, she had many falls at her home and at different times broke each of her arms, and got a cut on her head requiring stitches. But she didn't let anything stop her. She continued to garden and take care of her home. She hated giving up her car at age eighty-seven, but knew it was time.

It was getting more difficult for Mom to live alone, but she didn't want to move. As it turned out, she agreed to move into the little apartment in my lower level in 2010.

Me, my daughter, Jennifer, and my mom in 2009.

That apartment had been a source of both extended family quarters as well as rental property and extra income over the years. Now that apartment would become home for Mom. We worked hard to clean out her house, organized a garage sale to sell many of her possessions, and got the home ready to sell. Then we moved Mom's remaining possessions into my apartment. I continued to work, but we had dinner together several evenings a week, and I did her washing and helped her dress.

Mom had never really understood bank statements. She got Social Security, and that was what she lived on. Because my name was now on her bank account, I paid her bills and reviewed her bank statements. My brother and I could never convince Mom that she had more money in the bank than just her Social Security. She simply wouldn't believe that she had more than the amount of that check to spend. She wouldn't believe us when we tried to show her the bank statements which showed that whatever money she hadn't spent during a particular month remained in her account for her to use and she didn't have anything to worry about. But she was afraid that the bank would discover that they had made a mistake, and she continued to be frugal.

Mom still liked to feel somewhat independent and she liked to walk outside and enjoy my garden. When it rained, she would sit on a glider in the garage and watch and listen to the rain. She especially liked to watch the butterflies in my garden, and to this day every time I see a butterfly I think Mom has come back to say hello. I thoroughly enjoyed having her live with me, and we grew close again. We had to move Mom into a hospice center just three weeks before she passed away.

I had never been in the presence of someone at the time of their death. So, Mom's death was a totally unexpected experience. I was called to the hospice center by the nurses late in the morning of Wednesday, September 21. I was told that her breathing had slowed and it wouldn't be long before she died. I hurriedly called my brother who lived in Council Bluffs, Iowa, and told him to get here as fast as he could. I then drove to the hospice center to be with my mom one last time.

As I arrived, her two sisters were already there, talking to her in low voices as Mom lay in bed covered up to her neck with her favorite quilt that said "Mother." I hugged Maggie and Flora, and we held hands when the nurse came in and explained to us what would happen. We were waiting for my brother. We each spoke to Mom, leaning in close to her ear. She was not responsive, so we couldn't tell if she heard us, but we all wanted to say goodbye and that it was okay for her to go. We each felt that she knew we were there with her. We cried as we told her how much we loved her.

My brother soon arrived. It was almost noon. We noticed that her breathing was slowing down. Tom also spoke to Mom. Then the four of us joined hands, stood around her bed and sang her favorite hymn, "In the Garden." We

Mom and me in 2000.

quietly and reverently prayed the Lord's Prayer over her. Mom then took a final breath and was gone to her forever home. I never imagined my first close encounter with death could be described as beautiful, serene and soothing, but it was. Her sisters, Tom, and I were all comforted that we had been able to say goodbye and ease her passing.

Just as I had a sort of "other worldly" experience when I learned my daughter was pregnant with my first grandchild, I had another such experience after Mom died. It was just two days after her death and the weekend of my high school fiftieth reunion. I went to the social gathering on Friday evening, but didn't stay long. A friend of mine walked with me back to my car, parked in a garage downtown. When I got to the car, a rosary and a cross were hanging on my driver's side mirror. I looked around but didn't see any such ornaments on other cars. I believe in angels and had the strangest inclination that this was a sign from my mother in heaven, saying that she was okay and I didn't have to worry about her. To this day, I believe that, and I have that rosary and cross hanging from the mirror in my car. I will never remove it. I miss her very much.

What I know For Sure

The Joy of Solitude

I know for sure that we all need quiet and stillness so we can listen to our internal voice. After the past two hectic decades of my forties and fifties, I was finally able to realize something I had missed or misunderstood my whole life— the joy of solitude. As I noted earlier, I am a Pisces and always have needed a time of solitude in my regular routine.

In my younger days, however, I didn't think it was an acceptable personality trait to need solitude. I thought I was just a shy person who really didn't like to be around people very much. I felt the longing to spend time by myself was something I simply had to learn to overcome. It took me many years and a lot of reading and life experience to understand my need for periods of solitude in order to be able to enjoy and feel comfortable being sociable.

I worked with many groups of people in my business career and got along well with professional colleagues. Eventually, as I came to understand myself and my needs, I realized that the reason I could interact with others in a professional setting so easily was because I always had a "part" to play, as in a theatrical production. I was an office manager, an administrative assistant, a bookkeeper, and a secretary—even an editor of professional papers. But in each of those jobs I was following a script, doing what I knew the job called for. Thus, I could relate to others; we could discuss processes and the best way to get things done, etc. I was even quite comfortable in front of large groups leading meetings, because I was an actress reading from a script, playing a part.

I enjoy being around people, but usually with a specific part to play or with an end in sight. During my marriage I had tried, mostly unsuccessfully, to carve out alone times for myself. But I found that difficult to do with a child to raise, especially with a husband and father who rarely spent time alone with his daughter. So, I learned to enjoy my few minutes of solitude when I drove in my car to work or if I came home early in the day with my daughter in school and husband at work.

That is not to say that I am anti-social. I actually enjoy being around people, but mostly in small groups. During most of my life I have tried to avoid social conventions like cocktail parties or going to bars where social chit-chat is required. I prefer having deep and meaningful conversations with a few close friends and discussing the important issues in our lives and how we could help each other.

I enjoy many activities in solitude. In my Carriage Glen retirement community, I like to exercise in the community exercise room by myself with only natural light coming in the window and no radio or TV blaring. I review ideas in my head and think about what I might want to say in an article I'm writing. I also enjoy sitting on my covered deck while listening to the gently falling rain—and inhaling the wonderful calming smell it brings, reading, or listening to music with the sounds of the wind or the birds in the background. These kinds of solitary activities allow us to draw away from the needs of society and other people and focus only on ourselves for a moment.

One of my favorite solitary activities is walking in nature, with nothing in my ear to distract me. I really don't understand people who jog or walk with an earbud in their ear to block out all the outside noises. I think it's sad that people can't just be still and notice the beauty around them. I often talk to God as I'm walking and I focus on the beauty and sounds of nature all along the walking trail in my neighborhood—the sound of water flowing and falling over a waterfall in a large pond, the wind calling through the trees, the changing landscape of nature through the seasons, and the sounds of the critters. These solitary walks create pictures and stories in my mind and fill my soul with gratitude.

Do not be afraid to be alone; it's the only way you'll ever really get to know yourself. As Arthur Schopenhauer said in *Essays and Aphorisms*, "A man can be himself only so long as he is alone; and if he does not love solitude, he will not love freedom; for it is only when he is alone that he is really free."

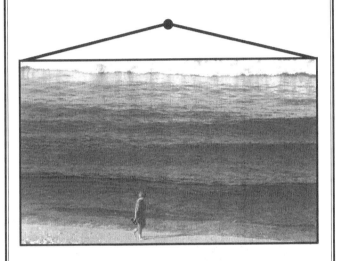

A solitary walk on the beach.

And on that note of self-discovery, my sixties were over. On to my next decade which would involve three major milestones and many new "firsts" in my quest to remain vibrant, active, open-minded and young-at-heart.

My Seventies—Dreams Finally Fulfilled

"Do not grow old. No matter
how long you live,
never cease to stand like curious children
before the great mystery into
which we were born."
—Albert Einstein

What I Know for Sure

We should not fear the aging process, nor should we "sweat the small stuff."

As so splendidly put by Shakespeare, "With mirth and laughter, let old wrinkles come." Aging is a part of our life's journey that many are not given the opportunity to experience. I don't believe we should be afraid of entering this phase of life, especially if we are lucky enough to have our health, sound mind, and mobility.

However, that's not to say that we should "go gentle into that good night" (as in the poem by Dylan Thomas) and accept limitations that we think come naturally with aging. We should never stop having dreams and goals for our lives—whether it be like mine to write a book, travel more, go back to school, or try something new such as tap dancing or quilting. Do whatever it is that makes you happy and feel alive.

As Elizabeth Gilbert said about her mother, who, incidentally, also was seventy-three years old at the time, in a Facebook post on March 29, 2016: "She was issuing a gentle warning not to fall into the trap of letting your life get smaller as you get older." That is a great visualization as to how some folks see aging—a narrowing of horizons, hopes, dreams, and activities. If possible, don't let that be the case for you.

When someone asks how I feel about turning a year older, I always reply, "It's certainly better than the alternative," and I am blessed to be able to experience growing older—and hopefully, wiser.

Along those same lines about growing older with no fear, I know that when you reach a certain age (and that age can vary depending on many factors) you will stop caring about "the small stuff" in your life and learn to concentrate on what is most important to you.

This has certainly happened for me in the past ten years. In my younger days, I used to be a "people pleaser." I really cared what people thought of me and I was afraid I might do something to displease others. I tried so hard to make people like me, to be the person that others expected, not to upset anyone by my words or actions. I almost lost my genuine *self* by letting others take control of my attitudes about fairness, truth, and even my likes and dislikes.

I no longer care what other people think about what I value and need in my life. I am now the central figure in my own life. I don't know how much time I might have left in this life to accomplish what is important to me. I do know that our time here is finite and must not be wasted on trivialities.

In 2013, I ran smack into another decade. Just three years prior, I turned another page on the aging calendar. I couldn't believe I was seventy because I still didn't feel old, and I was offended whenever someone referred to seventy-year-olds as "elderly." I felt that I had just come to another turning point for my life.

Since the sad episode of Ron's suicide in my early fifties, I felt like I had come a long way. I had learned many life lessons (things I know for sure) from the repercussions of verbal and emotional abuse suffered during my twenties, thirties and forties. After those defining yet difficult experiences, I had opened up my life and my mind to new ideas, expanded my horizons, turned my fear into excitement for new experiences and explored many new avenues of adventure. I was now the oldest member of my immediate family—the figure head, the torch bearer.

I began to yearn for something but I wasn't sure what it was. Peace? Contentment? New adventures? I didn't want to change my view of life as a beautiful adventure, full of wonder and awe, with inspiration and joy around every corner. I wasn't ready to sit back and just let life happen to me or pass me by. I was in good health, and I still wanted to be the captain of my own ship as long as possible, to steer my way through the sometimes turbulent, sometimes calm sea of my life's journey.

I started to think again about my moldy dream from my college days of actually becoming a writer. That idea had festered and moved ever forward in my brain for years while other important milestones were reached and surpassed. I'd resurrected that dream a few times with a new business and some individual writing projects, so I thought maybe it was time to resurrect it again.

I felt ready to thoroughly investigate some big changes for my life, i.e., new ways to make money, fully retiring and investigating retirement living options. These milestones were within my reach, and I just needed the courage and determination to follow through and find new waterways through which I could steer the final leg of my voyage.

Important Milestones Reached

The year 2015 was an eventful one for me. Three important milestones occurred in my life that changed the course of my future and led to the decision to write my life story and the lessons learned.

Leaving Church

The first major change occurred when I left my church home where I had been for seventeen years. Sadly, I slowly had discovered that, based on some of my deeply-held personal beliefs, I couldn't live a "true" life while remaining in that church. This was a heart-wrenching and difficult decision for me. I had many, many friends in my church home; but I felt I had no choice based on what I believed the Bible told me and some of the most important fundamental precepts of my spiritual beliefs.

Because I don't believe anyone has to agree with me, and many of my friends don't, I will keep most of my deepest personal beliefs to myself. In society today, we are too quick to condemn those who do not agree with us about abortion, the death penalty, gun control, politics or in many other areas of societal norms. I believe we do not have to agree in all areas of life in order to like and respect one another. Just because someone has beliefs that differ from yours does not make them racists, bigots, or any other names we hear discussed on the nightly news. There is too much name-calling and shouting in society today and not enough kindness, caring, and love for our neighbors.

"Real" Retirement

The second major change occurring in 2015 involved my professional work life. I had been working ever since I was eighteen years old. My first job was at Gold's Department Store in the men's department. So, I had worked for fifty-four years of my life. I had earlier retired from full-time employment at the University of Nebraska-Lincoln in 2000 when I was only fifty-seven years old.

However, because I still needed an income and I like to keep busy and feel useful, I continued to work part-time for the next fifteen years until the end of 2015 when I finally decided to quit work entirely. The main reason I decided to fully retire was because I was simply getting tired and wanted to have some time to try my hand at writing again, and because of the third major change in my life—selling my house and moving to a senior living community.

Moving to Senior Community

The third and biggest change in my life circumstance in 2015 was totally unplanned and unexpected. For twenty-five years I had been living alone in the same house I had purchased in 1990. Being a woman living alone, whose family had moved to another state half a country away, was becoming somewhat overwhelming for me. There were too many decisions to make. I couldn't find a reliable handyman to fix the many things that go wrong with older homes. Too many upcoming repairs were going to be needed—furnace and air conditioners (one of each for both my home and the downstairs apartment) and old appliances that could conk out at any time. However, though I knew those things were coming, I still hadn't thought about what living arrangement would be good for me.

I did know what my first choice would be because one of my good friends had moved into a small senior living community, called Carriage Glen, that I just loved when I visited her. However, I was sure I couldn't afford the entrance fee that was required. Then one day she invited me to lunch and told me that a one-bedroom unit had opened up, so she took me to see it. The moment I walked in, I knew I wanted this to be my next home. It was a large one-bedroom unit which I could choose to have painted any color I wanted, and I also got new carpeting throughout. So then and there, on the spur of the moment, I decided to put my house up for sale.

It was a good decision. In 2015, starter homes like mine were scarce on the market and were usually sold quickly for a good price. My house sold one day after it was listed in September—only two months after making the decision to sell my house and move to a totally different kind of living arrangement. I moved from a three-bedroom home into a three-room unit. I had to sell almost half of my possessions and gave many items to charity. And I am so happy about that decision. This is my motto these days: Less is more.

In my new home at Carriage Glen, most repair or maintenance decisions are taken care of by a maintenance team on site. The neighbors help each other out when

Moved into Carriage Glen; no more shoveling snow for me.

needed and with whatever talents each of them possesses. One of my neighbors helped me install my new wireless printer for my new computer. I felt liberated from all the decisions and repairs needed to keep a home running. I felt unburdened and free to fly, to travel, or to pursue what I've wanted my entire life.

I still live alone, but I have a family in my living community. It's small, just the way I like it, and I can be part of or apart from the activities that occur; it's my decision. This is the perfect living arrangement for me at this time in my life, and I am so lucky to have found it. In February each year, I can simply close the front door and turn into a "snowbird" moving to Florida for a month or two. I don't have to worry about my home because I know it will be looked after in my absence.

What I Know For Sure

A house does not a home make.

Since I sold my big house and moved to a smaller residence, I've learned that "a house does not a home make." I realize that I brought my home with me when I moved. I simply got rid of some of the "things" that clutter all of our lives. Many of my friends asked me if it was difficult to sell my house of twenty-five years. I couldn't take with me the big pieces of furniture because I was moving into a much smaller place. Others couldn't believe that it was so easy for me to change and uproot my life and leave my home. But I didn't leave my home.

I know it's difficult for some people to have to move from their homes to a smaller place or an independent or assisted living situation. But for me I was forced to realize and accept the fact that it's not the house that makes a home. My "home" *is* my family pictures and memories, the cards given to me each year by my daughter and grandkids, my collection of books and elephant statues, the souvenirs from my many travels, etc. A house is just a structure that contains a "home." These movable objects, for me, are what define my "home," and I take my "home" with me wherever I go.

Becoming a Writer

Because of all the changes in my life in 2015, my whole focus shifted. What I finally learned and accepted was that it was time to fulfill my dream of actually becoming a writer, and only I could do that.

I felt I would never be a fiction writer. I like to write non-fiction, short articles about memories or incidents in my life, about what it's like to grow older and about what I've learned throughout my life. I have always admired columnists like Erma Bombeck and writers like Anna Quindlen who have written about their life's journeys with self-deprecating humor, insights and worthwhile guidance for other women, both old and young.

So, when I was in Florida in February 2016, I spent two weeks by myself, and in that time, I had an outline for this book and started to work on the prologue. As I was writing, I knew I could also take some of my history and turn it into short articles. When I returned to Nebraska, I knew just how to start on my journey to be a columnist.

In Lincoln, we have a quarterly senior newspaper called *Lincoln 55+ Seniors Paper*. It's full of articles, columns and information of interest to our local senior community. I plucked up my courage, looked up the name and e-mailed the senior paper's editor with a sample of an article about my childhood to see if he might be interested in another columnist. His reply was swift and to the point: "I like this and will see if I can find room for a regular column. What shall we call the column? You are the first to write about Lincoln. Can you email me a head shot?" I was so excited I didn't know what to do. I called Marv, my daughter and my brother.

"I'm finally going to fulfill my dream to be a writer," I said to them all, "and it's only taken me fifty-three years!"

So, I have a column called "A Lincoln Life" in the senior quarterly newspaper. I also continued to work on this memoir. Increasingly I found myself writing and rewriting various articles and chapters of my book every day. I found it therapeutic to write about frustrating experiences I had, such as trying to solve a computer problem with a supposed "technician" over the phone when he only wanted to sell me a repair contract. I have made it a routine to write and/or rewrite something almost every day, except Sundays (and when I'm on vacation). After all, I needed to get a lot of experience writing in a short time, since it hadn't been a regular part of my daily routine since I was in college in the 1980s. Also, I didn't know how much time I would have left to express myself and leave a legacy for my daughter and grandkids.

One thing I have learned about being a writer is that it's not a good way to make money right away, and I'm sure only the most successful writers can earn a living at it. But at this point, I don't care; I am just so happy and fulfilled that many days I have to make myself get up from my desk and go for a walk because my back is hurting me as I sit hunched over my computer.

Discovering an Old Friend

In my first year in my retirement community, another amazing coincidence occurred involving a friend I hadn't seen in over ten years. I was still adjusting to my new environment and figuring out different ways of continuing to remain active. On this particular day, I was simply walking in a circle around my unit; it's an easy place to walk. For some reason, I happened to stop in front of my book shelves, looking at my various collections.

I pulled down a volume of Robert Frost poems and opened to the cover page. Inside was pasted a note from the person who gave me this gift, dated May 1983. The note said: "Thanks for everything you've done for me these last few months. If everyone had a friend like you, there would certainly be fewer problems to deal with in the world." It was from a friend, fifteen years younger than me, whom I had worked with at the UNL Water Center. At that time, she had been debating some personal decisions she had to make. We became close and had long heart-felt discussions about some fundamental beliefs involving the man in her life. I learned as much from her as she did from me.

I couldn't believe I had found that particular book with that particular note. At once I knew it was not just a coincidence, but a sign. I knew I had to call my friend. I looked up her number and noted that she had not moved from her old address. I immediately called her, and she told me later that she almost didn't answer because she didn't recognize my cell number. But we reconnected and talked for a very long time.

I discovered that she was again dealing with other issues involving the same man still in her life. I truly believe that some greater power led me to that book and that note at that particular time. I had been with her at the beginning of her relationship with this person, and now I was supposed to be with her again as she contemplated her future with him. I believe that God acts in mysterious ways and uses messengers and angels on earth to get our attention and to lead us in ways we are supposed to go to help others.

Since reconnecting with this old friend, I knew that we would continue to be connected as we both proceeded along our separate life paths, wherever they led us. As we age, old friends, as well as new friends, are so important; we should cherish and nurture these relationships. As we grow older, family and friends grow more essential to our own health and well-being. So, if you have a friend or friends that you haven't connected with in a while, call, e-mail or text them just to see how they're doing. Real friendships are rare and should be nurtured. Again, as with family, don't fail to tell your friends how important they are in your life before it's too late.

Other "Firsts" in My Life

In this decade of my life, I've also experienced many exciting new "firsts." I went out in public without a speck of make-up (yes, I'm one of those ladies—as was my mom before me—who wouldn't be seen in public without full hair and make-up). I also had my first pedicure because I always felt my feet were too ugly to be pampered. Well, not anymore. The pedicure was relaxing and I even took a picture of my painted toes and posted it on Facebook. I ventured out *alone* to an early movie and a late dinner also *alone*.

My most significant "first" in 2016 was my first close-up elephant encounter. Anyone who knows me knows that, besides my family and my writing, one of the greatest joys in my life is elephants—learning about them, watching movies about them, visiting them in zoos and collecting their likenesses. Of course, the biggest wish on my bucket list is to go on an African safari so I can see elephants in their natural habitat. While I haven't yet gone on a safari, this past summer I did the next best thing.

Have you ever been invited to or indulged yourself in a relaxing spa retreat with three of your friends? Well, that's what I did in the summer of 2016 during my first up-close encounter with my favorite pachyderms at Wilstem Ranch, an elephant sanctuary and growing safari park near French Lick, Indiana.

My three new friends were Makia, Lovie and Lulu, female elephants aged thirty-one to forty-two. For the first time that year, the three African elephants vacationed at Wilstem Ranch from mid-March until October 30. The elephant owners spent the other four months of the year with their elephant "children" in Sarasota, FL.

Elephant encounter at Wilstem Ranch, Indiana in 2016.

When the day arrived, I was a little apprehensive. Arriving at the ranch, there were a total of twenty participants in the elephant spa experience where we assisted in giving the three ladies their daily bath. The handlers explained that these elephants were now retired, but formerly had performed in the circus, marched in parades and attended state fairs. "Now," said the owner, "It's time for them to relax and pretty much retire." They spend four days per week interacting with elephant lovers in this fantastic spa encounter, and the rest of the time they are free to roam over their ten-acre environment.

I was the first of the group chosen to assist in bathing Makia. I got inside her pen and was handed a spray bottle filled with soap. I squirted and sprayed all over one side of her body. She stood calmly and tried to catch some of the spray in her mouth. The owners were always close at hand to teach and assist in the ritual. Too soon it was time for the next participant to take their turn. This process was repeated with each of the three pachyderms. Some of us got a second turn to help, and I was the last person to assist in rinsing off Lulu. Maybe they could see how much I wanted to be involved, or perhaps it was my big smile during the entire experience.

After the baths were finished, all three ladies were brought in together, and it was picture time. We got to reach up and touch the elephants, and the participants took turns taking pictures of each other with them. I had my picture taken with Makia, Lovie (who was born with only one tusk) and Lulu. I stroked their trunks and felt their skin which was stiff and scratchy. All the while, the elephants were docile, calm and receptive. It was obvious that they were used to being around people.

Participants were emphatically told that elephants really do not forget. In order for them to interact in this way, they must feel safe and protected. And if an elephant likes a particular individual, they will remember that person in a crowd. I certainly would like to witness this.

This truly was one of the most awesome experiences of my seventy-three years. I was reminded of the Dr. Seuss quote from *Horton Hears a Who*: "I meant what I said and I said what I meant, an elephant's faithful one hundred percent."

They are also the most awesome of creatures on God's green earth with many human characteristics. I have always felt an almost psychic connection to these large, lumbering, magnificent animals. I wish I could understand the reason for this strong connection.

What I Know For Sure

Do not be afraid to pursue happiness.

Finally, I've learned what makes me truly happy (like the sound of ocean waves that I can hear right now through the open door of my ocean-front vacation place). And I am not ashamed or afraid to go after what makes me happy, whatever it may be at any particular point in time.

I have learned not to make excuses for not having or not being able to pursue the things that make me happy. It is too easy to blame someone or something else for not getting what you want. All I can say is you will never get what you want if you don't take that first step. Your dream may not come true, but you have to make the effort. Have no regrets. Always try, try and try again. Never give up; never stop chasing your dream.

It only took me fifty years to realize my dream of actually becoming a writer. I tried different aspects of writing at different times of my life, so I actually made many starts and stops and starts again. But I've finally gotten to the place where I can call myself a writer and have seen some of my articles in print. That makes me happy and satisfied. I feel like I've at least accomplished one of my life's goals, as well as checking off another item on my bucket list.

Besides writing and being near the ocean, other things that really make me happy include

- The sound of my daughter's and grandkids' voices when they call me just to talk.
- Walking and listening to the sounds of nature.

- Elephants, looking at and reading about them and dreaming of seeing them in Africa.

- Enjoying a great meal using all my senses, i.e., the smell of fried bacon, the succulent taste of fresh fruit, and the sumptuous sight of a homemade cherry pie crafted with love.

- Enjoying my necessary times of solitude which replenish my soul and feed my mind.

I no longer fear change because, just like the four seasons, life is constantly changing, even if we may not recognize it at the time. I'm no longer afraid to change my mind or pursue new goals if my notion of "pursuit of happiness" changes, even if that involves doing something I've never tried before. I truly believe that my happiness is innately tied to my constant awe and wonder at the world around me. I have never lost that child-like enthusiasm for life. Others may believe I am naïve, but that child-like wonder is the most important part of what keeps my mind young and active and involved in life.

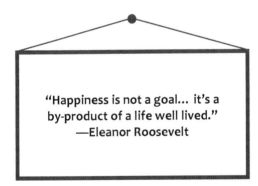

"Happiness is not a goal... it's a by-product of a life well lived."
—Eleanor Roosevelt

The Present

So, to sum up my life today, I feel good and am in good health. I've discovered the joy of exercise again, and I feel really blessed to be able to do pretty much what I want. It may take me longer to get out of bed in the morning, and I need to stretch my muscles before I begin my day; however, I feel blessed to have my health and mobility. Many of my contemporaries aren't so fortunate, so I try to never take anything for granted.

Our concept of aging and what it looks like has changed greatly over the years. I have a picture of myself with my daughter, my mother, and my grandmother, taken forty years ago when my daughter was about five years old. My grandmother looks different than today's version of a grandmother. I like to think I don't look my age. Perhaps that's just a misperception on my part—if that's the case, please don't tell me the truth. I like to dress fashionably (for someone of my age). I try to maintain my weight; and I actually have learned to enjoy walking and yoga.

From left to right: me, my Grandmother Kolb, Jenny, and my mom in 1978.

When I look at my women friends, we all look younger than our grandmothers looked when they were our age. Some are gray- or white-haired, but fashionably coifed; others color their hair. If they're lucky, most of my friends are still active. Some have overcome serious illnesses to be become better and stronger than ever. Women over sixty today seem to be more open to new experiences, to experimenting with new ideas, and to continuing to enjoy life—whatever that means to them individually. I do believe that unabashed attitude is a major component of aging gracefully.

There you have it. My life. My memoir—at least so far. I hope to have many more years of adventures and living ahead of me—if I'm lucky enough and with God's help to maintain my health and well-being. I recognize that I am not happy just sitting around. I need to be engaged in useful activities and helping others. That and my writing take up most of my time these days. Except, of course, for every February when I can be found on a beach, reveling in my favorite environment of sand, sea, and sky—listening to the ocean's roar, feeling its cold yet soothing touch on my toes, and absorbing the warmth of the sun on my face, as my body slowly relaxes and my mind is emptied of all cares. I simply savor those moments.

I am at peace. I am home.

The Sea

The sea is silent, serene, content.
Overhead, the sunshine creates diamonds in the water.
A fishing boat drifts lazily over the horizon.

All is as it should be —
The emerald and blue sea
waiting to awaken,
waiting for me.
I sit quiescent
listening to my muse.
Her never-ending melody
so alluring
so constant
so comforting.....
Not ready yet,
but waiting for me to return home.

Year after year
I return again to experience
the ever-lasting embrace of my eternal home —
the never ceasing, ever-revitalizing, immortal sea.

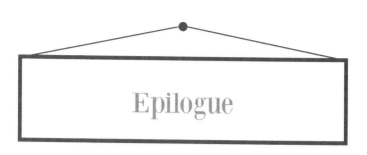

Epilogue

I HOPE YOU HAVE FOUND MY WORDS NOT pompous but perceptive; not inscrutable but enlightening; not simplistic but sensible.

The following quote summarizes most of the life lessons I've learned throughout my journey:

> *I'm stronger because I had to be,*
> *Smarter because of my mistakes,*
> *Happier because of the sadness I've known,*
> *And now wiser because I've learned.*
> *—Unknown*

I encourage you to find some similar mantra to which you can turn when the road gets rocky and you feel like you're sinking into quicksand. Just keep putting one foot in front of the other. Help others along the way wherever you are, however you can, with whatever you have. And give thanks every day for the simple joy of being alive.

I'm tired now and would like to go out for a walk on the beach as the fiery sun paints the clouds in pastel shades of pink, blue, and peachy orange. I want to witness the moon and stars rise in the darkening twilight to watch over each and every one of Earth's inhabitants for the night until the sun reappears and, hopefully, we will each wake again to continue our journey on this beautiful mortal coil for at least another day.

I leave you with a final Apache blessing, which I give to all my friends and to you, gentle readers.

May the sun bring you new energy by day,
May the moon softly restore you by night,
May the rain wash away your worries,
May the breeze blow new strength into your being,
May you walk gently through the world and know its beauty
All the days of your life.

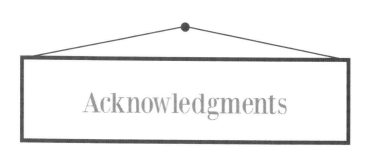

Acknowledgments

I WOULD LIKE TO ESPECIALLY THANK ALL my family, friends and my granddaughter who encouraged me in pursuit of my dream with good wishes, advice, suggestions, editorial assistance and in countless other ways.

My journey to become a published author would never have occurred without the invaluable assistance of the ladies at Concierge Marketing and Publishing in Omaha, Nebraska. They led me through all the various legal requirements, provided editing, artwork, and marketing help, and were always available whenever I had questions. Thank you for all your hard work on my behalf.

I also wish to acknowledge the assistance and advice of my significant other of nearly thirty years. Marv silently listened to me whenever I needed to discuss ideas or just clear my head; he was my confidant, my driver, my reviewer, my assistant in every way through this entire process. Thank you for always being by my side and for everything you've given me through our entire relationship.

About the Author

IN HER SOUL, KAREN HECKMAN STORK HAS always been an observer of the world around her. She loves quotes of all kinds, and views the world through a writer's eyes. Her mind conjures up "word pictures" for articles and poetry in the simple, ordinary places like Nebraska thunderstorms, a cardinal's visit to her deck, or a visit to Roca Ridge near Lincoln for a solar eclipse.

Karen calls herself "The Grandma Moses of writing" because it took her 53 years to achieve her long-held dream of actually becoming a published author. She began this current publishing journey in 2016 while spending a month in Florida in her favorite environment—the beach and the ocean. This is her sanctuary, her safe place where creativity flourishes.

While majoring in English at the University of Nebraska-Lincoln, Karen wrote many articles and poems which she still claims as some of her best work. Throughout her life she has been engaged in some form of writing, both work-related and personal. At one point she had a business called "Personal Verses" and wrote poems for clients to celebrate milestones in their lives. In 2008, she wrote and edited a publication for the University entitled "History of the UNL Water Center from 1964-2008."

Karen is a columnist for the *Lincoln 55+ Senior Paper*; her column is entitled "A Lincoln Life" because she has lived her whole life there.

Screw the Eggshells: Finding My Self After Verbal and Emotional Abuse is Karen's first publicly available book. She previously produced a family book entitled *Between the Generations: Poems by a Nana and her Grandson* in honor of their history of poetry writing.

Karen is a member of the Nebraska Writer's Guild. She is available to read from her book and speak to groups on subjects including the harmful effects of verbal abuse, aging without growing old, life lessons learned, and poetry. She looks forward to interacting with readers and can be reached through her website, www.KarenStork.com, where she writes a blog or at her email DiamondBeach@ConciergeMarketing.com.

Made in the USA
Lexington, KY
11 September 2017